MW00990823

Tasia's Table

Cooking with the Artisan Cheesemaker at Belle Chèvre

Tasia's Table

Cooking with the Artisan Cheesemaker at Belle Chèvre

TASIA MALAKASIS

PHOTOGRAPHY BY STEPHANIE SCHAMBAN

FOREWORD BY NATALIE CHANIN

NewSouth Books

Montgomery

NewSouth Books
105 S. Court Street
Montgomery, AL 36104

Text copyright © 2012 by Tasia Malakasis. Photographs copyright © 2012 by Stephanie Schamban.
All rights reserved under International and Pan-American Copyright Conventions. Published in the United States
by NewSouth Books, a division of NewSouth, Inc., Montgomery, Alabama.

Library of Congress Cataloging-in-Publication Data

Malakasis, Tasia.
Tasia's table : cooking with the artisan cheesemaker at Belle Chèvre / Tasia Malakasis ; photography by Stephanie Schamban.
p. cm.

ISBN 978-1-58838-272-6 (alk. paper) — ISBN 1-58838-272-9 (alk. paper)

1. Cheesemaking—Alabama. 2. Cooking (Cheese) I. Title.
SF274.U6M35 2011
637'.3—dc23

2012011758

Design by Valerie Downes

Printed by Pacom Korea
in Gunpo, South Korea

Contents

FOREWORD

By Natalie Chanin

I vividly remember the first time I saw Tasia Malakasis. It was a beautiful spring day and my company, Alabama Chanin, was hosting our annual picnic on the banks of the river that runs through our little town of Florence—Alabama, not Italy. Tasia walked up with a group of friends and a basket roughly twice her size full of cheeses and delicacies—all strikingly beautiful. Our community picnic and potluck was in full swing and there were incredible homemade dishes displayed down a long serving table. Tasia added her bounty and came over to introduce herself. We have been friends ever since.

I would like to say that I got my first taste of Chèvre de Provence (goat-cheese rounds marinated in extra-virgin olive oil and spices) that afternoon on the Tennessee River. But it was the following day, when the event was over and the guests had made their way home, that I found myself in the confines of my own kitchen with several unopened jars of Belle Chèvre. I made dinner by opening a jar and sitting it on my kitchen worktable with a package of crackers and some blueberries. I've never looked back. My first bite of that goat cheese-olive oil concoction set my head spinning and kept my mouth watering until I finally scraped the insides of the jar a day or so later.

That first jar led to a second jar and I decided to start adding it to my salads.

One day, as I was tossing together my salad, I found my jar virtually empty of the beautiful little rounds—all that was left was the oil and the crumbs of what I couldn't reach. In that moment, an idea came upon me: there, I thought, is my salad dressing. I squeezed a lemon into the empty container, shook it vigorously, and poured the mixture over a fresh garden salad, hoping the citrus would seek out and transport any remaining bits of magic to my plate. You will find the recipe on page 40. This is my favorite dressing (and I eat a lot of salad). Over the years, I have come to add garlic and just about every herb from my garden to the dressing. As Tasia says, the recipe is a "foundation for you to understand how you can improve it or make it your own."

The same with friendship. Tasia and I have grown our friendship across a few recipes and a couple of Alabama counties. I am proud to call her friend, supporter, colleague, and a daily source of inspiration. Truly incredible things do tend to come from those who are brave enough to follow their passions.

As we say in the South, "Dig in."

My Journey to Cheese

They say we are the sum total of our experiences. For most of us, that is quite a lot of stuff, some random, some planned. But if we are to "begin with the end in mind," do we ever really end up where we thought we would? I know I didn't. And for that I am truly glad.

When people ask me how I became a cheesemaker I jokingly say, "In the usual way." I think I am being clever because there is no usual path to becoming a cheesemaker. I am pretty sure there isn't a major one can declare for it, nor is it a vocational choice given to children, such as a fireman or nurse—at least not in the U.S. I didn't grow up, for instance, telling my first-grade teacher that I was going to be a cheesemaker. Honestly, I didn't even know something like that was a life choice when I was thirty, much less six.

The only thing I remember saying that I was going to be—and I felt a bit serious about this in high school, although entirely blind as to how I might accomplish it—was the first woman Chief Justice of the United States Supreme Court. I knew that it was a high aim, but I was always told that I could be anything in the world I wanted to be, and I believed it.

I studied English Literature in college not because I knew where it would lead but because I loved it. I was certain that if I got a good liberal arts education I could do anything I wanted. Anything. Cheesemaking still wasn't on the list.

I ended up building a successful and fast-paced career in internet technologies that challenged and kept me busy, but when I thought about what really made me happy, what I was really passionate about, it was, without a doubt, food and cooking and the simple act of sharing it with friends. Chefs were my heroes—the golden kind like Alice Waters and Daniel Boulud—and I wanted, I thought, to be like them, dedicated to making simple things elegant and more delicious than one can imagine.

That passion for food led me, mid-career, to the Culinary Institute of America (CIA). It was like being plugged in—how a new appliance must feel when it connects with power for the first time. Electric. I was surrounded by people whose sole purpose was to elevate and celebrate food, this source that keeps us alive, to an art form. I loved it!

So after what seemed like a professional attempt to deep dive into the food world, I still couldn't articu-

I can see now how my experiences have shaped who I am. I am an Alabama girl with a Greek heritage.

late what I wanted to *do* with this knowledge. Nevertheless, my passion for food, its mysteries, and its power only intensified.

While I was enrolled at the CIA, I went into Manhattan to my all-time favorite food store—Dean & Deluca—and was happily taking in the incredible bounty and variety of surreally beautiful foodstuffs. I wandered the aisles touching and smelling and exploring honeys and cookies and cakes and produce.

Then I stopped to linger over the marvelous cheeses from around the world. I picked up a goat cheese labeled Fromagerie Belle Chèvre, and on the label it proclaimed, "Made in Elkmont, Alabama."

The End. That's how I became a cheesemaker.

Okay, there is a little more in between that "chance" finding in Dean & Deluca and my becoming a cheesemaker, but that really was the moment—the time and place—where it all started.

After my stint at the CIA, I was lured back into my previous career, because even after culinary school and finding the cheese that was both renowned *and* made in my backyard, I still hadn't put two and two together.

I lived like this for some years more, on and off planes each week—sometimes with nanny and child in tow—

until I was finally ready to get off the merry-go-round. Then, despite knowing nothing about making cheese or the market into which it is sold and distributed, I called the founder of Belle Chèvre and said, "I just quit my job, and I'm coming home to make cheese."

All it took was everything

My favorite T. S. Eliot poem, "Four Quartets," which had no small part in luring me to where I am today, states in the most beautiful of ways that the exploration which seems like the end is really the beginning, "costing not less than everything."

Everything included quitting a job and leaving an industry I knew, getting a divorce, learning a new trade, buying a business (with very little resources), and finding a new home.

I can see now how my experiences have shaped who I am. I am an Alabama girl with a Greek heritage. I am a daughter. I was a wife, and I am a mother. I was an executive, and now I am a cheesemaker. I am a cook. And I am fortunate to call myself friend to many wonderful people who have guided me along the way.

All of these roles have been combined like one of my recipes to create me. Appreciable yet very ordinary. The "me" that is my experiences-to-date had a notion to write a cookbook to share what I love about my life as a cheesemaker, my recipes from my Alabama and Greek heritage, and my joy for playing in the kitchen.

It seems presumptuous of me to write a cookbook, which is really none other than a how-to book, especially since it comes from a woman who never really likes to measure anything. My hubris in trying to *teach* you how to do something that I most often make up as I go, or rather, as I am inspired, seems overreaching. I rarely ever follow a recipe; I find that my experiences often send me in slightly divergent directions from other cooking authors. Spontaneity and improvisation drive me in the kitchen—all with a nod to classic technique.

I am okay with this.

Not only am I okay with it, I heartily encourage it. My hope is that if I introduce you to a new recipe that I really have given you not one but ten new ideas on how to create a particular dish. Feel free to take any soup recipe you find here and substitute the vegetable for one you like better, or for something you just happen to have in the fridge. Take the technique of braising or the concept of frittatas and play with them. Create something that suits your own taste.

My son has a game he plays in the kitchen, something he has been doing for years, which is making a "potion." I put an extra-large mixing bowl in the sink and, as he stands on his stool to hover over it, he is allowed to put anything into that big bowl that he can find in the kitchen. Well, almost anything—I won't let him open a bottle of champagne! I normally end up acting the role of surgical assistant as he cries for soy sauce with his palm out waiting for it to be handed to him.

It isn't my hope for him to be a cheesemaker or a cook. My hope for him is that he will be creative and daring in all that he does. That would also be my hope for you with this cookbook, with these recipes serving only as a guide.

I have a tradition at my table. It is my personal take on saying the blessing or raising one's glass with a few words at the beginning of a meal. It is inclusive and communal, as everyone at the table or standing in wait for a buffet brunch is required to participate.

Homemade Goat Cheese

I submitted a recipe to *ReadyMade* magazine for making goat cheese at home. It truly is a fun thing to do. My goal with this cookbook is to have you realize how lovely and healthy and versatile goat cheese is—whether you make your own or use one of Belle Chèvre's goat cheese or any other goat cheese. I want you to enjoy and feel at home with this beautiful cheese! Note: Don't toss out the whey when you are done. Whey contains milk sugar, albuminous protein, and minerals. Leftover whey can be used as a liquid substitute in bread-making. Additionally it can be frozen to use at a later time.

Serves 2

1 quart goat milk

Juice of 1 lemon

Salt and pepper

Fresh chives, chopped

Cheesecloth or cotton kitchen towel

In a heavy-bottomed pot, bring goat milk to a boil over medium heat. Take off the heat. Immediately stir the lemon juice into the milk. Let stand for a couple of minutes, so the milk can curdle.

Lay out a cheesecloth (or a cotton kitchen towel) in a bowl. Pour in the milk-lemon mixture. The curds simply resemble curdled milk at this point so don't worry that they will pour right through the cheesecloth—it will catch them. Tie the ends of the cloth together so it becomes a bag. Hang it on a wooden spoon over the bowl or over your sink and let the bag hang free. The whey should strain out of the cheesecloth for at least two hours.

Before taking the cheese out of the cloth, squeeze the cloth to extract more liquid from the cheese. Transfer the cheese from the cloth to a bowl and season it with salt and pepper and fresh chives. Ready to serve.

It is also a sign of respect to the cook and to the abundance we are so very fortunate to have. At my house, around my table, we say "Three Things." Before the first fork is raised, everyone, whether it is only my son and I or thirty guests, goes in turn to say the three things he or she is thankful for.

Ever since my son could speak he has said his three things before eating. And always, to this day, it has been the same three things—"I am thankful for you, me, and the beautiful day."

I cannot recall the exact moment, but I believe the tradition of Three Things started at a time when I was reexamining my routine behaviors. I was a new mother of a young son and wanted to be very conscious of how he would grow up at the table—how the ceremonies of partaking of a meal could and would shape his life.

I had been particular, if not downright zealous, about food traditions for a long time before I became a mother, however. In fact, my thoughts and interests orbited around food well before I was self-aware enough to realize that *it* was my "passion."

Passion-driven pursuit

Calling my interest in food, and its tradition and culture, a passion is, I think, an adequate description. If passion is "a strong or extravagant fondness or desire," then that is my bent toward food. I learned early that food meant love. I learned this from my grandmother (as a lot of us do, no doubt). I dotted my early life's landscape with food-centric thoughts: cooking for my boyfriends' families—winning not just the boy's heart but the entire clan's—reading food-centric books, and following chefs and food writers in the same way that some teenagers follow rock stars. Yet I never thought about food as a career choice. I just didn't think that my "interest" could be coined as anything like a passion or a calling.

Now I am at home, both literally and figuratively, with my pursuit of food, with how it shapes my life and the lives around me, with the friends I have made, and how I have settled into this interest, this self-proclaimed passion. Beyond being comfortable with it, I hold sacred the power of food; how we share it shapes our world in ineffable ways. Through my journey I have become not only a mother concerned with her child's food traditions—like saying the Three Things—but a producer of a food item that is served at tables across the country. What a responsibility! What a beautiful responsibility.

When I first became a cheesemaker, I was asked what I ultimately wanted to achieve: what was my five-year plan, what was my goal? Those were great questions and ones that took a

My Food Rules

I have a friend that I fussed at so continually about "technique" that he now says, instinctively, after any recipe question, "I know, I know, it is technique!" Another friend will roll her eyes at me when she asks, "How long do I leave it in the oven?" She is searching for an exact time, and I will undoubtedly respond with, "Until it is done."

I am a firm believer that if one masters a few solid techniques then recipes will forevermore take a back seat to that concept of technique. If you know the technique for a great omelet, for instance, then you don't need a recipe—just creativity to put in whatever strikes your fancy. The same is true for techniques and principles of grilling, sautéing, braising, poaching, pickling, soup making, etc.

This book is a collection of some of my favorite things that I like to bring to the table to share with family and friends. It is my hope that if you learn how to make one of the frittatas in this book that you will have learned the "technique" to make any kind of frittata, limited only by your own creativity and availability of ingredients. My favorite cornbread recipe is a foundation for you to understand how you can improve it or make it your own by adding jalapeños, cheddar, or, of course, goat cheese.

My philosophy is *Food Is Fun*—being playful in the kitchen is a requisite to creating great memories at the table. Experiment with these recipes and have fun!

How I Use Goat Cheese at My House

Goat cheese is one of the most versatile cheeses on the planet. It's soft, easy to work with, and its mild flavor makes it perfect for use in a wide variety of dishes, from breakfast to dessert.

You can also feel very good about using it in various ways because of its unbelievable health benefits. Goat cheese is lower in fat and calories than cow's milk cheeses, higher in protein, lower in lactose, and actually supports a healthy digestive system. And if that wasn't enough, goat's milk is said to be good for your skin, hair, and even libido! Armed with all of that great information, I see very little reason for you not to enjoy it every day in more of your favorite dishes.

Here are few ways that I use it and substitute for the old stand-bys that call for:

1. Mayonnaise—Try a BLT with a delicious goat cheese spread on your bread instead of mayo. I use it on rustic French bread for my leftover Thanksgiving turkey sandwiches.

2. Sour Cream

3. Cream Cheese—My favorite shrimp dip now has goat cheese as its base instead of cream cheese. Add a healthy twist to cream cheese with pepper jelly dip by using goat cheese instead. Want a truly delicious cheesecake? You get the idea.

4. Butter—Crumble goat cheese on your favorite steamed veggies instead of butter; add a little lemon zest to it to make it even more special. Love a compound butter on top of grilled meats? Make herbed compound "butters" with goat cheese instead.

5. Make whipped cream by using half the amount of cream with goat cheese for a gourmet twist.

6. Spread goat cheese on your bagel with smoked salmon, capers, and red onion.

7. Use goat cheese in your icing for a favorite cake or cupcake.

good deal of thought to answer, because I had to ask myself, "Why am I doing this?" I became a cheese-maker primarily because it is fun. I find immense joy in it because it feeds me—both literally and figuratively—and because I get to share that joy with so many people through the products I create. Those are the same reasons I cook and share food at my table. At the beginning of a meal or even before, as I start cooking, I think of that wonderful gift.

The *why* in cooking is the most important starting point in choosing *what* to cook. The reasons are plentiful if you think about it—to romance, to love, to celebrate, to honor, to sustain, to share ideas. And then I ask myself which foods and settings will help me to arrive at that destination. My feelings about cooking are perfectly described in the Story People artists' collective "Real Reason" prints: "There are things you do because they feel right and they may make no sense and they may make no money and it may be the real reason we are here: to love each other and to eat each other's cooking and say it was good."

I start my days now in contemplation of foods and traditions that I—Southern first, American second, and somewhere in there Greek, too—enjoy. I also think about how you might start your day, what will happen around your table, and how I, the products I make and the recipes I share, get to participate in that. It is a magnificent thought that I may extend myself into your life and enjoyment of food just by crafting a product or sharing a recipe.

Before my tradition of Three Things, I still had a propensity for beginning a meal with some form of reverence. I would often read a poem at big, over-flowing meals at the lake, particularly "Perhaps the World Ends Here" by Joy Harjo. Harjo depicts every great moment of our lives taking place over a table. She shows how a table can bring people together in joy and sadness and closes with my favorite line: "Perhaps the world will end at the kitchen table, while we are laughing and crying, eating of the last sweet bite."

From the beginning of my day to the "last sweet bite," I will share with you in this book more than the traditions at my table, more than my stories of how I believe food shapes our lives: I offer you my life history through some of my favorite recipes. As you can imagine, quite a few of my creations will feature cheese, but as importantly, they will feature the region that I once couldn't wait to escape but eventually embraced wholly: it's my grandmother's legacy on my hands and now on your table.

Lastly, I am thankful for "you, me, and the beautiful day."

Bon appétit.

My favorite T. S. Eliot poem, "Four Quartets," which had no small part in luring me to where I am today, states in the most beautiful of ways that the exploration which seems like the end is really the beginning, "costing not less than everything."

Breakfast

I love beginnings. Beginnings are full of promise and a kind of energy that is hard to replicate. It is important to think of how, before you begin, you wish the end to look, to feel—and for us in the kitchen, to smell. The beginning of the day or the beginning of a meal is a sacred time and should be honored, even in small ways.

Breakfast is my favorite meal and one in which there is an infinite amount of creative room to play with traditional ingredients. I like to give the morning its due with a meal—a real meal. More often than not, what was enjoyed at the dinner table the night before finds itself reinvented at the breakfast table—the asparagus is now in my frittata, the potatoes and pork loin have been turned into a hash, chile verde is topped with a fried egg on a tortilla with chopped onion and cilantro. It is like being handed a palette of colors and you get to make a painting—even better, since the painting is edible, no?

I encourage you to sit down at the table and begin your day with good tastes and wonderful sustenance. I love breakfast so much so that if given my choice of any restaurant, it would most certainly be one known for its breakfasts. While I was in culinary school in New York, breakfast was the meal I did not miss—no matter how tired I was. All of the culinary students had to do a stint working in the breakfast restaurant. The breakfasts were nothing short of phenomenal and anything but standard. However, we had to report to work at 3 A.M. to start the prep for opening at 7 A.M. I was cured of wanting a breakfast restaurant after that experience, but not cured of seeking an incredible beginning meal.

Even though breakfast is my favorite meal, and even though I am armed with the knowledge that breakfast is the most important meal of the day, it is still tempting to hit the snooze button and skip or skimp on this meal. Nevertheless, my son and I sit down together at the breakfast table every morning—despite the sometimes hectic pace with which the school and workday may start—say our Three Things, and enjoy a good breakfast. I have vowed to not eat my breakfast on the run, in the car, or away from the smooth, worn edges of a table.

Weekends present another opportunity, however. On the weekends we linger over the breakfast table. I once started a breakfast club for the early rising neighborhood children who couldn't wait to start their Saturdays by knocking on my door at seven o'clock in the morning. We would invite them in and share our breakfast traditions—frittatas and eggs-in-a-nest and such. It grew into a "Are we having Breakfast Club this weekend, Ms. Tasia?" I really loved the sound of that question! Even better was when the gaggle of children scattered outside, leaving the leisurely weekend breakfast table still surrounded by the parents, an event often spanning all the way past noon. I am always pleased when just another pot of coffee is being made and conversations last until eventually someone asks, "What's for lunch?"

French Press Coffee with Steamed Milk

I have experimented quite a bit with different methods of brewing coffee. And spent quite a lot of money along the way. It seems indicative of my style to have to try everything but to eventually come round to champion the simplest method out there. This would be a twelve-ounce French Press, sometimes called

a "press pot." If you have never had coffee made in a French Press, I encourage you strongly to try it. It couldn't be simpler, and frankly I believe it couldn't be better. Café au lait is the French version of coffee with lots of milk, fifty-fifty coffee to milk. The milk is steamed or warmed. I no longer have any fancy coffee equipment in my kitchen, so I just gently heat my milk on the stove and boil my coffee water in an old teakettle that lives on my stove.

Serves 6

3 rounded tablespoons coarse-grind coffee

12 ounces boiling water

12 ounces warmed milk

Scoop 3 tablespoons of ground coffee into the bottom of the French Press. Slowly pour in the boiling water. Stir well with a wooden spoon. Put top of press on the container and let coffee steep for 3–4 minutes. Plunge slowly. Pour coffee into huge coffee "bowls" halfway and then fill with warm milk. Sweeten as desired.

Fresh-Squeezed Orange Juice

When I am in Greece and staying with my sisters at my stepmother Dina's house, the day always begins with a glass of fresh-squeezed orange juice. It is indescribably delicious.

I know that most of us won't take the time to do this every day, but for certain occasions it is absolutely worth it. A simple juicer makes it oh so easy.

There is an endless variety of presses and juicers on the market, and some of them are quite expensive. A very simple plastic one with a strainer to catch the seeds on the sides can work just fine. I have a rather *War of the Worlds*-looking one that I leave on the counter at all times, just in case the mood strikes.

Serves 1

4 large oranges

Per person, you need about four large oranges, cut in half.

Squeeze juice with your press or manual juicer directly into a glass. Enjoy!

Hot Cocoa

I don't know of a single child who doesn't love hot cocoa on a cold morning. For that matter, I don't know many adults who would turn down that offer. As a matter of fact, and I promise I am telling the truth, my son had hot chocolate with his breakfast this very morning. Pre-made mixes are certainly accommodating but I know you will find them lacking in comparison to this easy-to-create recipe. A little tip for the coffee drinkers: after amply handing this out to children, I sometimes spoon the remaining cocoa from this recipe into my coffee cup instead of steamed milk.

Serves 2

3 cups whole milk

1 cup half-and-half

¼ cup good quality Dutch-process cocoa powder

½ cup sugar

¼ teaspoon cinnamon

¼ teaspoon pure vanilla extract

Marshmallows, for topping

Pour milk and half-and-half into a saucepan and bring to a simmer over medium heat. Meanwhile, stir together the cocoa powder, sugar, and cinnamon. To make a smooth paste, stir the hot milk into the cocoa mixture a few teaspoons at a time. Scrape the cocoa mixture into the saucepan with the milk and simmer a few minutes; do not let it boil. Stir in the vanilla.

Pour into small serving cups and place 4 marshmallows on each serving. Serve immediately.

Mimosa

You know that orange juice you just squeezed? I have just the perfect thing for you to do with it!

A Mimosa is a classic breakfast or brunch drink, and honestly I cannot think of a better friend for an orange than a sparkling wine. I was just recently in the region in Italy where Prosecco reigns. Prosecco was served everywhere and for every occasion—don't you love the Italians?—and especially at breakfast. Prosecco was even on the breakfast buffet at our hotel. Since it is having a moment here in the States, feel free to try it or any other sparkling variety that you love in making a Mimosa.

Serves 4

8 ounces orange juice, preferably fresh-squeezed

1 (750-milliliter) bottle champagne or Prosecco

Champagne flutes

Pour 2 ounces of orange juice into each flute. Fill almost to the rim with champagne. Toast and celebrate the day!

Bloody Mary

The Bloody Mary is one of my all-time favorite drinks. I love it especially because it is so savory and spicy (my preference), and I adore it in a salt-rimmed glass (my second preference). Inevitably when I think of a Bloody Mary it conjures images of New Orleans and brunch at Commander's Palace . . . or just Sunday suppers at my house. I serve mine with lots of accompaniments such as pickled okra, olives, celery stalks, and anything else pickled I have around. And salting the rim is always a nice touch. It is also a lot of fun to put out a Bloody Mary bar since everyone is their own Bloody expert. Customization can be accommodated with ease, and experimentation is encouraged. I will make up a delicious base mix and then put out a beautiful array of options.

Serves 6

Mix

32 ounces (1 large container) V8 juice

6 ounces premium vodka

Half a large lemon, juiced

Generous shakes of salt and pepper

4 large dashes Worcestershire sauce

4 large dashes hot sauce

Bar Ingredients

Pickled okra

Celery stalks

Fresh horseradish

Pimiento-stuffed olives

Hot sauce

Lemon or lime wedges

Set Up

Large glasses

Ice

Let everyone assemble their own and customize as they choose. This leaves your hands as cook and host free to entertain.

DIY Breakfast Cheese

We use Belle Chèvre's fromage blanc for our recipe (*fromage blanc* is a soft, often spreadable goat cheese), but if you cannot find it in your stores, you can use a goat cheese log moistened with milk or cream until it is a spreadable consistency. The amount needed will depend on how dry the log is.

Serves 4

1 cup fromage blanc

2 tablespoons honey

Mix the fromage blanc and the honey. Serve on your favorite breakfast bread. Enjoy!

Belle and The Bees Stuffed French Toast

A perfect breakfast or snack, this is a more nutritious version of French toast. Lightly sweetened goat cheese is the surprising, delicious filling for sweet bread. Strawberries add some freshness to the honey-flavored goat cheese, tucked in the toasty bread.

Serves 4

4 slices (about 2-inches-thick) dense bread, like challah

4 ounces Belle & The Bees Breakfast Cheese (honeyed goat cheese)

8 strawberries, sliced

2 tablespoons butter

1 cup buttermilk

3 large eggs

1 tablespoon sugar

½ teaspoon lemon zest

¼ teaspoon cinnamon

⅛ teaspoon salt

Cut the bread slices almost in half, leaving one edge intact to form a pocket, similar in appearance to pita bread. Spread the cheese on the inside of each piece. Follow with a layer of strawberries and close the bread.

Heat pan over medium-high heat. Melt butter in pan. Whisk the buttermilk and the remaining five ingredients in a flat bowl. Dip the bread into the mixture, soaking sides and edges. Fry in pan until each side is golden brown.

Keep warm in a 250-degree oven while preparing remaining French toast in the same way.

Breakfast Quesadillas with Smoked Salmon and Goat Cheese

The quesadilla is a go-to item in my house. Sometimes it is simply cheese that is toasted between two beautiful tortillas and served as a snack. This recipe is certainly an elevated example. You already know what I am going to say but . . . feel free to experiment once you are comfortable with the technique!

Serves 6–8

1 small red onion, thinly sliced crosswise

11 ounces goat cheese, room temperature

2 teaspoons fresh chives, finely chopped

½ teaspoon fresh lemon zest, finely grated

¼ teaspoon black pepper

Breakfast Suggestions

For a quick but very fulfilling breakfast, imitate the Mediterraneans and serve cheese and fruit and slices of cured meats (salami, for example). The breakfast table at my family's house in Greece always has a hunk of feta on it.

Other breakfast ideas using goat cheese include serving it on toast with honey or jam or whipping it into biscuit recipes instead of buttermilk.

A great way to get vegetables to the table in the morning is to combine them with your eggs in a frittata, omelet, or scrambled eggs.

With the addition of a tortilla and some sour cream, non-traditional breakfast meats, such as braised roasts or even shredded chicken, can creatively turn scrambled eggs into a delicious Mexican-inspired dish.

12 (8-inch) flour tortillas (not low-fat)

1 pound smoked salmon (preferably Nova), sliced

1 firm, ripe California avocado

2 teaspoons lime juice, freshly squeezed

3 tablespoons extra-virgin olive oil

1 pound (2⅔ cups) cherry tomatoes, halved lengthwise

Soak sliced onion in a bowl of ice and cold water 15 minutes; drain well and pat dry.

While onion soaks, stir together cheese, chives, zest, and pepper in a bowl until well combined.

Evenly spread about 1½ tablespoons cheese mixture over 2 tortillas (keep remaining tortillas covered with plastic wrap). Top one tortilla with an even layer of salmon, covering goat cheese completely; then top with other tortilla, cheese side down. Make 5 more quesadillas in same manner, then stack on a plate, cover with plastic wrap, and chill until ready to heat.

Halve, pit, and peel avocado, then cut lengthwise into ⅛-inch-thick slices. Lightly brush avocado slices with lime juice and set aside.

Heat cast-iron skillet over high heat until very hot, then reduce heat to moderate. Lightly brush 2 quesadillas on both sides with some oil, then toast on skillet (one at a time if necessary) until undersides are golden with some blackened spots, about 1 minute. Flip quesadillas over with a spatula and toast until undersides are golden with some blackened spots, 1–2 minutes, then transfer to a baking sheet, arranging in one layer, and cover with foil to keep warm. Toast remaining quesadillas in same manner, using a second baking sheet.

Heat remaining oil in the same skillet over high heat until hot but not smoking, then cook tomatoes, stirring occasionally and seasoning with salt and pepper, until they just begin to soften, about 1 minute.

Transfer quesadillas to plates, then top with onion, avocado, and tomatoes.

Spring Pea and Goat Cheese Frittata

Frittatas are my easy go-to breakfast dish. In fact, I will go for periods where I make them almost every morning for my son and myself. When I told him I was going to write a cookbook, Kelly immediately said, "You should put in our frittatas! You're the one who made them up!" I am the only author of the frittata in my son's mind, but you can be the author of your own version very, very easily. You can make them with almost anything you have on hand. The base ingredients are eggs, milk or cream, and some kind of cheese. Once you get the technique and concept down there is no stopping you from an endless variety of frittatas.

Cook's note: What is left over from the previous night's dinner is normally what ends up in the breakfast—asparagus to roast chicken come back alive in this simple baked omelet with a great Italian name.

Serves 4

2 tablespoons olive oil

1 leek stalk (light part only), thinly sliced

½ cup fresh peas, blanched and drained

6 large eggs

1 small bunch fresh mint, stems removed, torn into small pieces

What's Love Got to Do with It?

At home, when you make those favorite cookies (or other special dish) that you meticulously copied down the recipe for while your grandmother (or other special person) whipped them up for you, do they taste the way you remembered?

Whole companies are inspired by grandmothers' secret recipes, and internationally renowned chefs (even and especially the surly ones who have boastfully elevated food to high art) credit their grandmothers' humbler hearths as their inspirations; when asked about those original childhood food moments, eyes roll back just a bit and smiles slowly spread across serious faces as food is recalled that was lovingly made for us alone, with results that often can't be replicated.

One of my best girlfriends tells me often about her childhood spent in her grandparents' basement kitchen (I never knew why the kitchen was in the basement) watching the preparation of all kinds of masterful Italian dishes. She made meatballs with her grandmother, who schooled her on how the meat should feel as it is kneaded—like a woman's breast, her grandmother would say. My friend now will spend the better part of a day recreating that recipe. She is proud of the way the meatballs turn out, but she still admits they don't taste as good as in her grandmother's basement kitchen. Why is that?

I think about this mystery a lot. In fact, I talk about it a lot in relation to the recipe we use to make our cheese at Belle Chèvre. Ours isn't a secret recipe, as the making of goat cheese is a relatively simple exercise, but I confidently believe that our cheese tastes the way it does because of how we make it, because of the emotion and the pride we put into it when we are making it, and—please forgive the sentimentality of this—because of the love with which we make it.

I feel silly in a way writing about this because it seems so trite to say.

Kung Fu Panda learns that there is no secret in the secret recipe.

Before I had any ideas of formulating this mystery into a theory I went so far as to say that my grandmother's chicken and dumplings would be a memory that I wouldn't muddy. My grandmother was my definition of love, and she tangibly and magically whipped her love into a round fluffy form we all know as a biscuit. But that biscuit wasn't just a biscuit and even my eight-year-old self recognized that.

I vowed quite some time ago *not* to try to emulate her chicken and dumplings, nor do I eat anyone else's. I realize that stance is probably over the top, but it is where I am with protecting that particular memory and that particular kind of love.

Kosher salt and pepper, to taste

2 ounces goat cheese, crumbled

½ cup half-and-half

Preheat oven to 425 degrees.

Heat the oil in a large ovenproof sauté pan over medium heat. Add leek and sauté until soft, then add peas and cook for 2–3 minutes more.

Meanwhile, in a medium bowl, beat the eggs with ½ cup of half-and-half.

Add the eggs and half the mint to the pan, season with salt and pepper, and cook, lifting the edges with a spatula to allow the uncooked eggs to flow to the bottom. When the frittata is partly cooked (7–10 minutes), sprinkle on the goat cheese and transfer the pan to the oven.

Bake for 8–10 minutes until puffed and golden. Remove and allow to cool slightly. Garnish with the remaining mint to taste and serve.

Perfect Fried Eggs

Serves 1 or 2

2 teaspoons butter or olive oil (or bacon grease)

2 large eggs

Salt (fine sea salt preferred) and pepper

Place a 7- or 8-inch nonstick frying pan (I like a well-seasoned cast-iron pan) over medium heat and add butter. When the butter has foamed and the foam begins to subside, carefully break and slip the eggs into the pan. Reduce the heat a bit and cook slowly until the whites are firm, about 3 minutes. Use a nonstick spatula to turn the eggs over gently. Let them cook on the second side for about 30 seconds. Carefully lift the eggs out of the pan and place on warmed plates. Season to taste with salt and pepper.

Fried Eggs and Learning to Cook to Please

I kind of see fried eggs the same way that Forrest Gump's friend Bubba saw shrimp. There are so many ways to enjoy them—fried egg sandwich, fried egg on a tortilla, fried egg on sautéed greens with bacon. I have even had a fried egg on a pizza and served on a bowl of steaming soup!

My mother always made the fried eggs when I was growing up. Saturday mornings were filled with sounds of eggs cracking against the side of the skillet and then landing, sizzling, on the hot surface. One morning I wanted to make them—create for myself those splendid sounds and the resultant oozing yellow on the plate—and I received my first fried egg lesson. She told me I did a good job (a wonderful thing for a girl to hear from her mother), and I suppose it was true because from then on it was my job to fry the eggs. I didn't take this job lightly because my mother liked her fried eggs just so. The yoke had to be runny but the whites absolutely cooked through, and with one flip.

I didn't find it easy to achieve the perfect fried egg, and sometimes this task would produce no small amount of anxiety. There was so much that could go wrong! The yoke could break just after entering the pan (maddening!) or during the flip. The whites might not be all the way finished when the yoke starts to harden—that is *not* good. It makes me nervous just to think about it!

I most often use butter or olive oil but my mother always fried eggs in the grease left in the pan after frying bacon. It produces a very obvious smoky flavor for the eggs, and little flecks of bacon are seized in the egg whites that make them very delicious. If you aren't concerned about the fat, then please use bacon grease for a wonderful treat.

Sweet Potato Hash

I love the idea of a hash for breakfast, even though the corned beef hash seen on most menus tends to scare me a bit. I will often make a hash the morning after I have made a delicious roasted pork loin, and cube several thick leftover slices to put into the hash. If you don't have a pork loin to use, bacon is a good substitute—or, for that matter, any rustic roasted or grilled meat.

Serves 4

4 sweet potatoes (1¾ pounds), peeled and cut into 1-inch pieces

2 tablespoons extra-virgin olive oil

6 ounces slab bacon, sliced ¼-inch thick and cut into ½-inch pieces

1 pound Vidalia or other sweet onions, cut in a rough dice

2 tablespoons parsley, chopped

½ teaspoon dried oregano

2 tablespoons chives, minced

Salt and pepper

In a medium saucepan of salted boiling water, boil the sweet potatoes for 3 minutes; drain well.

In a large skillet, heat the oil. Add the bacon and cook over moderate heat until crisp, 4–5 minutes. With a slotted spoon, transfer the bacon to paper towels to drain. Add the onions to the skillet and cook over moderate heat until browned, about 12 minutes.

Add the sweet potatoes and cook over moderate heat, stirring occasionally, until just tender, about 15 minutes. Increase the heat to high and cook without stirring until browned on the bottom, about 2 minutes. Stir in the bacon, parsley, oregano, and chives.

Season with salt and pepper and serve with your Perfect Fried Egg on top. A little crumble or two of goat cheese and herbs on top of that, and you are in heaven.

Egg in a Nest

This is one of the neighborhood children's favorite things to ask for when coming to Ms. Tasia's house, no matter what time of day. Little Jack Schamban swears by mine, but just know that it is the easiest recipe to make and has a little bit of fun built right in. I make these one at a time, and if you have a crowd you can keep the prepared ones in a very low heat oven (you don't want to cook the yolk through) until all are made and everyone is gathered at the table.

Serves 1

Olive oil (to coat the bottom of the pan, may need to add again after the flip)

1 slice good-quality whole-grain bread

1 egg

Sprinkle of salt and pepper

Coat the bottom of a good nonstick or, even better, a cast-iron skillet with olive oil. Heat over medium heat.

Use a biscuit cutter or just free-form tear a hole in the center of the bread.

Place holey bread in skillet and crack the egg in the hole. Let the egg set up and the bread get toasty on one side and then flip to toast the other side of the bread for roughly 2 minutes per side, depending on preference for how well done the egg should be. I believe it is best though when the yolk is runny and can spread over the plate so the bread can soak it all up!

Belle Chèvre Scrambled Eggs with Shiitake Mushrooms

Who doesn't love scrambled eggs? If there is someone out there who doesn't, I haven't met her. This recipe is a hearty and earthy way to dress up the standard fare.

Serves 4

3 tablespoons butter, unsalted

6 ounces shiitake mushrooms, stems removed, caps thinly sliced

Salt and pepper

8 large eggs, well beaten

3 tablespoons chives, snipped

3 ounces (about ⅓ cup) mild goat cheese, crumbled

Toast, for serving

In a large nonstick skillet, melt 2 tablespoons of butter. Add mushrooms, season with salt and pepper, and cook over moderate heat, stirring occasionally, until softened and lightly browned, about 5 minutes.

In a bowl, season the eggs with salt and pepper. Melt the remaining butter in the skillet with the mushrooms; add the eggs. Cook over moderately low heat without stirring until the bottom is barely set, 30 seconds. Add the chives and cook, stirring occasionally, until the eggs form large soft curds. Remove from the heat and sprinkle the cheese on top; let stand until softened, 30 seconds. Gently fold the cheese into the eggs; serve with toast.

Belle Chèvre Baked Eggs

I first fell in love with baked eggs at my friend Lyn Aust's wonderful gourmet bistro in Huntsville, Alabama. Hers were ultra-yummy, as I recall, with ham and spinach. This is a simple yet very elegant version. What I especially like is that it is remarkably easy to feed a crowd with this dish.

Serves 6

2 tablespoons mixed fresh herbs (parsley, basil, thyme, mint, tarragon), chopped

Clove garlic, minced

2 tablespoons butter, melted

2 tablespoons heavy cream or half-and-half

6 eggs

3 tablespoons goat cheese, finely crumbled

Sea salt

Cracked black pepper

Preheat oven to 450 degrees. Combine herbs and garlic; set aside. In a glass measuring cup, mix butter and cream. Place six 4-ounce ramekins or ovenproof cups on a baking sheet. Pour butter mixture evenly among ramekins. Bake in oven until bubbly hot, about 1–3 minutes.

Remove from oven. To avoid breaking yolks, carefully crack 1 egg into a separate cup and gently slide it into a heated ramekin. Top eggs with herb and mixture and crumbled cheese. Sprinkle with salt and pepper. Repeat with remaining eggs.

Return to oven and bake 3–5 minutes. Eggs should look not quite done; they will continue to cook after removed from oven. Place each ramekin on a plate. Serve immediately with toast.

Cornmeal Pancakes Topped with Honey-Pecan Butter

I wholeheartedly agree with Mark Bittman, author of *How To Cook Everything*, when he said that we must have, as Americans, lost our connection to the kitchen when we stopped making pancakes from scratch. This recipe calls for an incredibly easy mix of ingredients, and I am sure you will love experiencing the result. The fromage blanc makes it especially pleasing.

I adore this recipe!

Serves 4–6

Honey-Pecan Butter
½ cup (1 stick) butter, unsalted, warmed to room temperature

2 tablespoons honey (my favorite is Savannah Bee's Tupelo Honey)

¼ teaspoon cinnamon, ground

⅓ cup toasted pecans, chopped

Salt, to taste

Cornmeal Pancakes

1 cup plus 2 tablespoons all-purpose flour

⅓ cup fine yellow cornmeal

2 tablespoons sugar

1 teaspoon baking powder

½ teaspoon baking soda

¼ teaspoon salt

2 large eggs

¾ cup fromage blanc

¾ cup whole milk

¼ cup vegetable oil

½ teaspoon vanilla extract

Melted butter

Maple syrup, warmed

Using electric mixer, beat butter, honey, and cinnamon in small bowl until fluffy. Stir in pecans. Season with a touch of salt. Set aside honey-pecan butter for serving with pancakes.

Combine flour, cornmeal, sugar, baking powder, baking soda, and salt in large bowl. Whisk eggs in medium bowl; whisk in fromage blanc, milk, oil, and vanilla. Gradually add liquid mixture to dry ingredients, whisking just until blended.

Heat griddle or heavy large skillet over medium heat.

Working in batches, brush griddle lightly with melted butter. Pour batter by ⅓ cupfuls onto griddle. Cook until bottoms brown, about 4 minutes. Turn pancakes over and cook until second sides brown, about 2 minutes. Divide pancakes among plates and top with honey-pecan butter. Serve, passing warm maple syrup separately.

Christmas Breakfast Strata

Every year we do a Christmas breakfast at my house, and unlike my tree which gets decorated differently each year, the breakfast remains the same. This is a  classic strata recipe from my Southern memories (a "strata" is often a layered egg-and-bread dish). I prepare it the night before and bring it out of the fridge to come to temperature as the wrapping paper and shouts of surprise (real and obligatory) are flying around the living room. This recipe is an easy one for brunches or breakfasts any time of year when you have company. The wonderful part is that it feeds a crowd and can be assembled ahead.

Serves 6–8

1 pound pork sausage

6 1-ounce slices good French bread, cubed

1 tablespoon green onions, chopped

2 cups cheddar (or a mixture of any cheeses you have on hand), shredded

6 eggs

2 cups milk

1 teaspoon salt

1 teaspoon dry mustard, ground

Place sausage in a large, deep skillet. Cook over medium-high heat until evenly brown. Drain and set aside.

Layer sausage, bread cubes, cheddar, and green onions in a lightly greased 7 x 11-inch baking dish. In a bowl, beat together the eggs, milk, salt, and mustard. Pour the egg mixture over the bread cube mixture. Cover, and refrigerate at least 8 hours or overnight.

Remove the casserole from the refrigerator 30 minutes before baking. Preheat oven to 350 degrees.

Bake 50–60 minutes in the preheated oven, or until a knife inserted in the center comes out clean. Let stand 10 minutes before serving.

Biscuits

I remember that my grandmother had a special bowl for biscuits. I didn't realize at the time that a lot of ladies in the South did as well. And for most making biscuits required no measuring—the amounts were mysteriously known, just as they all somehow knew how much hairspray to use to hold their hair till next week's beauty parlor appointment.

I lived with my grandmother for a short time and she would make these biscuits ahead of time and freeze them. Before school she would pop them into a warmed oven so that we could have a treat on the run to meet the bus.

Serves 4

¼ cup shortening

2 cups self-rising flour

⅔ cup buttermilk

Cut shortening into flour with a pastry blender or fork until crumbly. Add milk, stirring just until dry ingredients are moistened.

Turn dough out onto a lightly floured surface, and knead lightly 3 or 4 times. Pat or roll dough to ½-inch thickness; cut with a 2-inch round cutter, and place on a lightly greased baking sheet.

Bake at 475 degrees for 10–12 minutes or until golden brown.

Pumpkin Bread

I love breads like this for breakfast, but the impetus for this particular recipe was that my son fell in love with a pumpkin bread from a local bakery. I couldn't be happy about this, so I set out, in a very competitive way, to make a better version.

Outside of my own need to please and be praised for my cooking, breads of this type are wonderful for breakfast with a smear of a creamy breakfast cheese on top.

Serves 8

3½ cups unbleached all-purpose flour

2 teaspoons baking powder

2 teaspoons baking soda

1½ teaspoons salt

1½ teaspoons ground cinnamon

¾ teaspoon nutmeg, ground

3 cups (about 24 ounces) canned pure pumpkin

1 cup sugar

1 cup (packed) golden brown sugar

1 cup fragrant extra-virgin olive oil (sounds strange, but trust me)

4 large eggs

1 teaspoon fresh ginger, peeled and minced

¾ cup buttermilk

Confectioner's sugar for dusting

Preheat oven to 350 degrees. Grease two 4½ x 8½-inch loaf pans with butter or nonstick spray.

Combine flour, baking powder, baking soda, salt, cinnamon, and nutmeg in medium bowl; whisk to blend. Using electric mixer, beat pure pumpkin and both sugars in large bowl until blended. Gradually beat in oil, then one egg at a time, then minced ginger. Stir in a fourth of the dry ingredients, followed by a third of the buttermilk; repeat until dry ingredients and buttermilk are both mixed in. Divide batter among prepared pans.

Bake breads until tester inserted into center comes out clean, about 1 hour. Cool in pans. Sprinkle generously with confectioner's sugar. If made one day ahead, cover; store at room temperature.

Soups, Salads, and Sandwiches

It is the middle of the day that always gets me. I find myself hungry and I rarely have a plan for this liminal time period between the beginning and end of the day. I enthusiastically anticipate and plan breakfasts, brunches, and dinners and their accompaniments, but always seem to neglect the middle-of-the-day meal called lunch.

The good thing about that is that these three items—soups, sandwiches, and salads—lend themselves very well to improvisation and relentless creativity. So if you find yourself like me and it is high-noon without a thought or a plan in the world for what you might make to eat, you are in luck. With some basic staple pantry items and whatever you have on hand, you can conjure up an infinite variety of lunch options. I strive to always have on hand chicken stock, fine quality bread, and some kind of leafy green. This way no matter what form of bread or green or stock I have, I know that I can, without much difficulty, either when company arrives or just to curb my own temporary starvation, whip up a soup, sandwich, or salad in some form or another. Invariably, I always come up with a new idea, or three, just from sheer necessity—you

know what they say about her as a mother. And I love the idea of the three of these foods as siblings or best friends who all love to play together, but somehow one of them always gets left out and a duo forms—soup and sandwich, or soup and salad, or salad and sandwich—you get the idea.

Soups have been a source of comfort for me since well before I can remember. I have the triumvirate of influences when it comes to soups: my grandmother, my mother, and, of course, Campbell's.

My grandmother, in all her love and goodness, made soups for me. Oftentimes they were delivered on a tray down to the dock from which we dove and swam around and under until our water-soaked, ravenous fingers were as crinkled as the Ruffles chips that might accompany the soup and sandwich. Those

Chicken Noodle Soup

This is the simplest of recipes and one of the most rewarding. I find that some days I cannot have anything else other than a good bowl of chicken noodle soup. My mother made it for me when I was growing up and ever since soups have been my most treasured comfort food. My Greek stepmother taught me the added dimension that the touch of lemon gives.

Serves 8

2 tablespoons extra-virgin olive oil

1 medium onion, chopped

3 cloves garlic, minced

2 medium carrots, cut diagonally into ½-inch-thick slices

2 celery ribs, halved lengthwise and cut into ½-inch-thick slices

2 teaspoons dried oregano

1 bay leaf

2 quarts chicken stock, recipe follows

8 ounces dried wide egg noodles

1½ cups cooked chicken, shredded

Kosher salt and pepper

Squeeze of lemon

Place a soup pot over medium heat and coat bottom with oil. Add the onion, garlic, carrots, celery, oregano, and bay leaf. Cook and stir for about 6 minutes until the vegetables are softened but not browned. Pour in the chicken stock, and bring the liquid to a boil. Add the noodles and simmer for 5 minutes until tender. Fold in the chicken, and continue to simmer for another couple of minutes to heat through; season with salt and pepper. Squeeze a few drops of lemon juice just before serving.

Corn Soup

This is a simple and beautiful summer soup. Serve this soup hot or chilled. You can make this soup even more delicious by adding chopped cilantro, diced avocado, or tomato. You can take it one step further and really make it fancy by topping it with crabmeat or grilled shrimp.

Serves 6

10 ears sweet corn

2 medium onions, chopped

1 tablespoons vegetable oil, olive oil, or butter

1 teaspoon salt, plus more to taste

1 medium potato, chopped

4 cups water, or chicken or vegetable broth

Cilantro, chopped (optional)

Avocado and tomato, diced (optional)

Using a large hole grater over a very large bowl, grate off the corn kernels. Use the blunt side of a knife blade to scrape remaining liquid and corny bits into the bowl. Set aside this luscious raw corn purée.

Chop onions. In a large pot heat oil or butter over medium heat. Add onions and ½ teaspoon salt. Cook, stirring occasionally, until onion wilts, about 3 minutes.

Meanwhile, peel and chop potato. Add potato and water or broth to pot. Bring to a boil. Cook until onions and potatoes are very soft, about 10 minutes. Add corn. Cook until heated through, about 2 minutes.

Purée with an immersion blender, blender, or food processor. (Do this in small batches to avoid splashes and burns.)

Add salt to taste. Garnish with cilantro, avocado, or tomato, if you like.

Chilled Pea Soup

Serves 6

8 slices bacon

1 tablespoon extra-virgin olive oil

2 celery ribs, thinly sliced

1 onion, thinly sliced

1 leek, white and tender green parts only, thinly sliced

5 cups chicken stock or low-sodium broth

Salt and white pepper

2 (10-ounce) boxes frozen baby peas

¼ cup flat-leaf parsley leaves

2 ounces goat cheese, crumbled

In a medium-sized soup pot, cook the bacon over moderate heat until browned and crisp, about 6 minutes. Transfer the bacon to a plate. Pour off the fat in the pot.

In the same pot, heat the olive oil. Add the celery, onion, and leek, and cook over moderately low heat, stirring occasionally, until softened but not browned, about 7 minutes. Add the chicken stock, 4 slices of the cooked bacon, and a pinch each of salt and pepper. Simmer until the vegetables are very tender, about 10 minutes. Discard the bacon. Using a slotted spoon, transfer the vegetables to a blender. Reserve broth.

Meanwhile, bring a medium-sized saucepan of salted water to a boil. Add the frozen baby peas and parsley, and cook until just heated through, about 1 minute; drain. Add the baby peas and parsley to the blender, and purée until smooth, adding a few table-spoons of the broth to loosen the mixture. Transfer the purée and remaining broth to a large bowl set in a larger bowl of ice water to cool.

Ladle the chilled pea soup into bowls, and top with the crumbled goat cheese. Crumble the remaining 4 slices of bacon into each bowl and serve.

Goat Cheese Salad Dressing

Serves 6

4 ounces goat cheese, room temperature

2 teaspoons lemon juice

½ teaspoon lemon zest

1 teaspoon Dijon mustard

Pinch superfine sugar

2 tablespoons low-fat (1½ percent) buttermilk

Salt and white pepper

1 scallion, chopped

In a small bowl, stir the goat cheese, vinegar, mustard, and sugar until smooth. Stir in the buttermilk and 2 tablespoons of water until smooth; if necessary, stir in more water. Season with salt and white pepper. Stir in the scallion just before serving.

The dressing can be refrigerated, covered, for up to 3 days.

Natalie's Tuscan Chèvre Salad

Natalie Chanin, a renowned fashion designer from Florence, Alabama, and a dear friend of mine, came up with this delicious recipe as a simple and inspired creation for a main course salad. Her talents, as you will be able to taste, go far beyond the art of textile.

Serves 4

4 handfuls fresh salad mix

1 cup cherry tomatoes

2 leftover grilled chicken breasts

Belle Chèvre Tuscan Chèvre (goat cheese marinated in oil with herbs)

½ lemon, juiced

Pepper, to taste

Place jar of Tuscan Chèvre in bowl of hot tap water to warm. Slice cherry tomatoes in half, lightly salt, and set aside. Slice chicken breasts into one-eighth-inch strips, and set aside. Wash and dry greens. Fill one-half of a plate with greens and add salted cherry tomatoes.

Fan chicken slices on other half of plate. Spoon warmed goat cheese on top of each slice of chicken, centering the cheese on each slice. Remove remainder of goat cheese from jar and place in bowl to be

Salad—Not Boring Anymore

As a good Southern girl, it took me a while to really appreciate a good salad. For the longest time I had an impression of people who ate salads as people who didn't really like food but were looking to order something healthy from the menu, as they were on a strict regime towards eventual disappearance. Of course, I had this opinion because I was always the one ordering the extra-cream-laden bisque with a full entrée to accompany it. I never stopped to think that my choices might have seemed excessive.

One day in the not-too-distant past I wrote to a friend who always raved about salads that a change had occurred in me. I liked salads! I realized I was the one who wasn't being creative.

Now I always keep some sort of greens in my fridge—kale, spinach, green leaf, even iceberg—so I can whip up a fantastic meal of a salad based on whatever other ingredients I have on hand. Not only has my opinion of people who eat salad changed, but my opinion of salads has changed.

I was limiting myself from amazing options, and I am so glad that salads and I are not boring anymore!

eaten at the table.

Spoon oil and "goodies" from the jar (sun-dried tomatoes) over chicken strips topped with cheese. Place additional crackers on the table to enjoy with the remainder of your Tuscan Chèvre.

For the dressing, add juice from one-half lemon and pepper to taste to the remainder of oil in jar. Close lid and shake. Pour dressing over salad and eat.

Frisée Salad with Lardons and Baked Chèvre de Provence

Serves 4

Goat Cheese Rounds
4 discs marinated goat cheese from 2 jars of Belle Chèvre de Provence (goat cheese in oil with herbs)

2 cups breadcrumbs, toasted

Salad
6 ounces slab bacon, rind discarded if necessary and bacon cut into ⅛-inch-thick slices, then cut into 1-inch-wide pieces (to form lardons)

1 tablespoon olive oil

2 tablespoons shallot, finely chopped

2½ tablespoons sherry vinegar

½ teaspoon sugar

¼ teaspoon salt

1½ pounds dandelion greens, stems and center ribs discarded and leaves cut into 2-inch pieces (10 cups)

Spread breadcrumbs on flat surface. Roll goat cheese rounds in breadcrumbs, then bake on oven rack in middle position at 375 degrees until warmed.

Prepare salad while goat cheese rounds bake. Cook bacon in a 12-inch heavy skillet over moderate heat, stirring occasionally, until browned and crisp, about 12 minutes. If necessary pour off all but 1 tablespoon fat. Add oil and shallots to skillet and cook, stirring, until softened, about 2 minutes. Add vinegar, quickly stirring and scraping up brown bits; then stir in sugar and salt. Immediately pour hot dressing and bacon over dandelion greens in a large bowl and toss well.

Divide salad among plates and put a warm goat cheese round alongside each salad. Serve immediately.

Watermelon, Red Onion, and Goat Cheese Salad

Serves 4

2–3 cups watermelon in bite-sized chunks, seeds removed

2–3 ounces goat cheese, crumbled

¼ large red onion, thinly sliced

2 tablespoons balsamic vinaigrette dressing, recipe below

2–3 tablespoons fresh basil, chopped

Balsamic Vinaigrette
3 tablespoons balsamic vinegar

2 tablespoons fresh lemon juice

1 tablespoon Dijon mustard

½ cup olive oil

In large salad or mixing bowl, gently toss all salad ingredients except the basil. When ready to serve, top with basil.

Whisk first 3 vinaigrette ingredients in medium bowl to blend. Gradually whisk in oil. Season dressing to taste with salt and pepper.

The dressing can easily be made ahead of time. Rewhisk before serving.

Salad of Gratinéed Goat Cheese with Sesame-Honey Dressing

This salad was inspired by one I had on vacation in Europe. The flavors are incredible, with the sweet-tangy dressing and sun-dried tomatoes playing off the warm, creamy goat cheese. I could eat this at every meal.

Serves 4

Salad

4 cups mixed greens (I like raddichio, mixed baby greens, and arugula)

¼ cup pine nuts

1 cup sun-dried tomatoes

1½ cups water

½ cup apple cider vinegar

8 ounces goat cheese

⅓ cup sesame-honey dressing (see below)

Sesame-Honey Dressing

6 tablespoons oil

2 tablespoons cider vinegar

1 tablespoon honey

2 tablespoons Dijon mustard

2 tablespoons sesame seeds, toasted

Clove garlic, minced

Sea salt and pepper

Heat the water and vinegar to nearly boiling, and add the sun-dried tomatoes. Rehydrate for at least 15 minutes. Then remove from water, pat dry, and drizzle with olive oil (optional).

Preheat oven broiler. Break up goat cheese into a glass baking pan and place under broiler until cheese browns in spots.

Meanwhile, toss greens with a sprinkling of salt, pepper, and the dressing to taste. Divide greens, nuts, and tomatoes between four plates, then top with hot goat cheese.

Combine all ingredients but sesame seeds in blender. Blend until smooth. Then add sesame seeds, and blend until incorporated. Pour into small jar and refrigerate any leftover dressing.

Greek Kiss with Tomato Salad (for the Grill)

Serves 6

6 Greek Kisses (Belle Chèvre goat cheese wrapped in grape leaves; see receipe on page 54 to make your own)

¼ cup extra-virgin olive oil

2 tablespoons balsamic vinegar

2 teaspoons Dijon mustard

6 large tomatoes, thinly sliced

⅓ cup (about 30) pitted oil-cured black olives, coarsely chopped

6 ½-inch-thick slices crusty country-style white bread

Prepare barbecue (medium-high heat). Whisk ¼ cup extra-virgin olive oil, vinegar, and mustard in small bowl to blend. Season dressing with salt and pepper. Slightly overlap tomato slices on large platter. Drizzle with dressing; sprinkle with half of olives.

Place Greek Kisses on grill, seam-side down. Grill until cheese softens and leaves begin to char, about 2 minutes per side. Arrange cheeses atop tomatoes. Sprinkle with remaining olives.

Brush bread slices with remaining thyme oil. Grill bread until beginning to brown, turning occasionally, about 5 minutes. Cut toasts diagonally in half. Serve cheese, passing toasts separately.

Beet and Belle Chèvre Salad

Nothing goes together better than the two earthy flavors of beets and goat cheese.

Serves 4

4 medium beets, scrubbed and trimmed, leaving about 1 inch of stems attached

Vinaigrette

1¼ teaspoons Dijon mustard

2 tablespoons white-wine vinegar

¼ teaspoon dried tarragon, crumbled

¼ teaspoon salt

¼ teaspoon black pepper, freshly ground

¼ cup plus 2 tablespoons extra-virgin olive oil

Herbed Goat Cheese

¾ cup fresh breadcrumbs

½ teaspoon dried tarragon, crumbled

¾ teaspoon salt

⅛ teaspoon black pepper, freshly ground

8 ounces Montrachet or other soft goat cheese, cut into 8 ½-inch rounds and chilled, covered

2 bunches watercress, coarse stems discarded, rinsed and spun dry (about 8 cups)

Preheat oven to 400 degrees.

Wrap beets tightly in foil and roast in middle of oven 1–1½ hours, or until tender. Unwrap beets carefully and cool until they can be handled. Discard stems and peel beets. Cut each beet into 8 wedges.

Beets may be prepared up to this point 1 day ahead and chilled, covered.

Make vinaigrette. In a blender, blend together mustard, vinegar, tarragon, salt, and pepper. With motor running add oil in a stream, and blend until emulsified. Vinaigrette may be made 1 day ahead and chilled, covered.

Make herbed goat cheese. In a bowl stir together breadcrumbs, tarragon, salt, and pepper. Cut each cheese round in half, crosswise. Coat each piece of cheese evenly with crumb mixture, pressing gently, and transfer to a baking sheet. Goat cheese may be prepared up to this point 1 day ahead and chilled, covered loosely. Let cheese come to room temperature before proceeding.

Toss watercress, onion, and half of vinaigrette into a bowl. Arrange watercress mixture, beets, and goat cheese on 8 salad plates and drizzle remaining vinaigrette over beets.

Belle Chèvre's Croque-Monsieurs

Serves 4

3½ ounces (½ cup) mild goat cheese, room temperature

4 tablespoons olive oil

8 ⅓-inch-thick slices French bread, cut on the diagonal so that each slice is about 3 inches long

In a small bowl, cream together the goat cheese and 1 tablespoon of oil. Spread 4 slices of bread with the mixture and top them with the remaining slices, pressing the sandwiches lightly. In a small nonstick skillet, heat 1½ tablespoons of the remaining oil over moderately high heat until it is hot but not smoking. Sauté 2 of the sandwiches for 1½ minutes on each side, or until they are golden, and transfer them to a plate. Sauté the remaining 2 sandwiches in the remaining 1½ tablespoons oil in the same manner.

Three-Cheese Grilled Cheese— with a Little Soul

Serves 4

8 slices French bread, cut on diagonal (about 3 inches long and ⅓-inch-thick)

1 cup (packed) whole-milk mozzarella, grated

4 teaspoons fresh thyme, minced

8 tablespoons Parmesan, freshly grated

4 tablespoons goat cheese, crumbled

4 thin slices smoked ham

4 tablespoons (½ stick) butter

Arrange 4 bread slices on work surface. Layer each with ¼ cup mozzarella cheese, 1 teaspoon thyme, 2

tablespoons Parmesan, 1 tablespoon goat cheese, and 1 ham slice. Top each with bread slice.

Melt 1 tablespoon butter in heavy large skillet over medium-low heat. Add 2 sandwiches to skillet. Cover and cook until bottoms of bread are golden and cheeses are melted, about 2 minutes. Add 1 tablespoon butter to skillet. Turn sandwiches over; cook until bottoms are golden, about 2 minutes longer.

Transfer sandwiches to plates. Repeat with remaining butter and sandwiches.

My Southern Basil Pesto

I always have tons of basil in my garden. If I haven't eaten it all by the time it goes to flower I gather it all up and make a bunch of pesto, freezing the reserves for the winter.

A good Southerner, I substitute pecans for the traditional pine nuts. It is even more delicious that way.

Serves 4

1 cup basil leaves

¼ cup pecan pieces, toasted

⅓ cup Parmesan, freshly grated

Clove garlic, crushed

½ cup olive oil

Sea salt

To make the pesto, process the basil, pecans, Parmesan, garlic, oil and salt in a small food processor until combined.

Mushroom, Pesto, and Goat Cheese Sandwiches

Serves 2

1½ ounces butter

8 ounces button mushrooms

Sea salt and cracked black pepper

2 sourdough rolls, halved

3 ounces goat cheese

My Southern Basil Pesto (see recipe on page 46)

½ cup Swiss cheese, grated

Heat the butter in a large nonstick frying pan over medium heat. Add the mushrooms, salt, and pepper, and cook for 5–8 minutes or until brown. Set aside.

Spread rolls with pesto and goat cheese, top with the cheese and grill (broil) under a preheated hot grill for 1–2 minutes or until the cheese is melted and golden. Top with the mushrooms to serve.

Goat Cheese with Eggplant and Roasted Peppers on Olive Bread

Serves 1

1–2 ounces goat cheese (herbed or plain)

2 slices olive bread or any rustic country bread

1 medium eggplant cut into 3 ¼-inch-thick slices

½ large red pepper (or jarred roasted red pepper)

1 teaspoon lightly salted butter

Thinly slice eggplant, brush with olive oil, sprinkle with salt and pepper to taste, and grill or broil for 4–5 minutes.

Hold peppers over a flame until blackened. When cooled, peel, discard skins, and place peppers in a paper bag.

Spread goat cheese on one side of bread. Place eggplant and pepper on the other piece of bread. Close sandwich. Evenly spread ½ teaspoon of butter onto each slice of bread. Grill over moderate heat for 3–4 minutes.

Chèvre Is a Sandwich's Friend

Many years ago on the day after Thanksgiving, I was doing what I normally do, which is not participating in Black Friday but participating in the art of enjoying leftovers with my sisters. I have always enjoyed turkey sandwiches with extra helpings and slathers of mayonnaise but substituting, as I am sometimes prone to do, goat cheese for the mayonnaise. The result of that substitution makes me so happy that I have never gone back to mayonnaise on my sandwiches. The goat cheese is not only lighter and healthier, but it creates a wonderful creamy and tangy flavor that I can now no longer live without.

Try goat cheese on all of your sandwiches—ham and turkey, BLT, egg salad. We have even stirred PB&J into the goat cheese for a much better than Nutella sensation!

Black Olive Tapenade and Goat Cheese Wraps

Serves 4

Goat Cheese Spread

1 pound goat cheese

¼ cup heavy cream

2 tablespoons thyme leaves, chopped

Place all the ingredients in a bowl and stir to combine. Set aside.

Tapenade

1 cup pitted Kalamata olives

2 anchovy fillets

2 teaspoons capers packed in brine, rinsed and drained

½ teaspoon garlic, smashed (use the edge of a large, wide-bladed knife)

Place all of the ingredients in a food processor fitted with the metal blade, and process until finely chopped. Transfer to a bowl. Set aside.

Wraps

8 flour tortillas, 10 inches in diameter

2 roasted red bell peppers, halved

2 cups frisée, coarse ends trimmed, curly tips torn into pieces

Lay the tortillas on work surface. Spread ¼ cup of goat cheese over the center portion of each tortilla. Spread 1 generous tablespoon of the tapenade over the goat cheese.

Cut each pepper half into 6 strips, and lay 3 strips along the center of each tortilla. Top the pepper with some frisée.

Fold two sides of the tortilla over the frisée, then roll up the tortilla. Cut each wrap crosswise into 4 pieces and serve from a platter.

Potato, Greens, and Goat Cheese Quesadillas

Serves 4

1⅓ cups potatoes (about 2 of medium size), Yukon Gold, peeled and ½-inch cubed

2 teaspoons chili powder

1⅓ cups (packed, 5–6 ounces) hot pepper Monterey Jack, coarsely grated

1⅓ cups salsa verde (tomatillo salsa), prepared

4⅔ cups stemmed mustard or collard greens (from 1 bunch), coarsely chopped and divided

4 flour tortillas, 8 inches in diameter

3 ounces goat cheese, coarsely crumbled and chilled

Olive oil

Place baking sheet in oven and preheat to 275 degrees. Steam potatoes until tender, about 8 minutes. Place in large bowl. Sprinkle with salt, pepper, and chili powder. Toss to coat. Cool potatoes 15 minutes. Mix in Jack cheese. Meanwhile, blend salsa and ⅔ cup (packed) greens in mini processor until greens are finely chopped.

Arrange tortillas on work surface. Divide remaining greens between the bottom half of each tortillas. Top greens with potato mixture, goat cheese, and 2 tablespoons salsa mixture, each. Fold plain tortilla halves over filling, pressing to compact. Brush with oil.

Heat large nonstick skillet over medium heat. Place 2 quesadillas, oiled side down, in skillet. Brush tops with oil. Cook until quesadillas are brown, about 3 minutes per side. Transfer to sheet in oven to keep warm. Repeat with remaining 2 quesadillas.

Cut each quesadilla into 3 or 4 wedges. Serve with remaining salsa.

Appetizers

I often think just as hard about what to serve guests as they arrive as I do about the main course. The appetizer is the prelude to the meal and sets the tone. Casual weeknight meal, dinner party, Sunday supper, or chili night with friends all need a fun way to engage the group, get the event started.

I was recently at a very nice restaurant in south Florida and one of the appetizers that came to the table for our crowd was a large bowl of popcorn scented with truffle oil and finely grated Parmesan. It was a fun and elegant setting and the tone that that appetizer set was lively and engaging as the bowl was passed around the table. I loved the creativity of the simple snack being elevated to elegant.

And that is a great way to think of starters or appetizers for your meals—easy ingredients that can be quickly elevated with some unique additions.

It all depends on the event, but unless I have a more formal occasion, I tend to keep appetizers close to the action in the kitchen.

We all know that the kitchen is where everyone wants to be so even if I am serving lunch outside, or dinner in another part of my home apart from the kitchen, I like to have everyone where the action is to start things off. While pots are bubbling in the background I will set out on the counter or table close to the kitchen snacks that all can enjoy before the meal.

I am a little selfish and want to entertain while entertaining and not be apart from it all. And I think your guests or your family—whoever is over for dinner—want to see what is going on around the stove and that that in its own way is part of the party.

Our notion of entertaining is vastly different today than it was in the 1960s and '70s when I was growing up. Even architecturally, kitchens are now open and an integral part of living and dining areas are no longer hidden away. Look at restaurants today where you can pay extra to sit in the kitchen with the chefs, at the Chef's Table and watch all of the action. Engagement in the activity and action of cooking (sights, sounds, and smells) is in my mind part of the appetizer—the whetting of the appetite for all the goodness yet to come.

Cheese Plate

Cheese is the easiest and perhaps most elegant appetizer. Simply taking it out of the fridge, warming to room temperature, and arranging on a platter with simple garnishes is a delicious way to start an evening event or an effortless snack for when a few close friends drop in.

Try to include a mix of fresh, aged, soft, and hard cheeses, arranged in the order in which they should be tasted: from the lightest and freshest to the ripest and most intense.

Serves 6–8

4–6 ounces goat cheese or fromage blanc

4–6 ounces aged cheese, such as Manchego

4–6 ounces ripened cheese, such as Brie or Camembert

4–6 ounces washed rind cheese, for a bold taste (I like Red Hawk by Cowgirl Creamery.)

Add an assortment of garnishes such as olives, honey or honeycomb, nuts (almonds, spiced pecans, etc.), and of course some yummy bread and crackers.

Arrange on a slate board or a wonderful, old and distinguished cutting board for an elegant display.

Spiced Pecans

Spiced pecans are another Southern party snack. They typically find themselves on the bar for you to enjoy while eagerly awaiting your cocktail. I like to have them on hand for a quick snack, too, when friends pop in.

Serves 20

1 teaspoon kosher salt

½ teaspoon cumin, ground

½ teaspoon cayenne pepper

2 pounds pecan halves

4 tablespoons butter, unsalted

¼ cup (packed) light brown sugar

2 tablespoons (packed) dark brown sugar

2 tablespoons water

Line a half sheet pan with parchment paper and set aside.

Mix the salt, cumin, and cayenne together in a small bowl and set aside.

Place the pecans in a 10-inch cast-iron skillet and set over medium heat. Cook, stirring frequently, for 4–5 minutes until they just start to brown and smell toasted. Add the butter and stir until it melts. Add the spice mixture and stir to combine. Once combined, add both sugars and water, stirring until the mixture thickens and coats the pecans, approximately 2–3 minutes.

Transfer the nuts to the prepared sheet pan, and separate them with a fork. Allow the nuts to cool completely before transferring to an airtight container for storage. Can be stored up to 3 weeks.

Pimiento Chèvre with Saltines and Celery

Did you hear that Joel Stein of *Time* magazine declared 2011 the year of pimiento cheese? Every dog has his day, I suppose. But what Joel perhaps didn't know is that in some geographies and communities in the South, pimiento cheese has had more than its day; it is a long standing staple.

Since I am a goat cheesemaker and a Southerner, I thought I would try my hand at a modern version. We liked it so much at the creamery that we began to market it. This version is doing quite well out there in the world.

If you cannot find it on your own grocery store shelves then here is the recipe to whip it up at home.

Serves 4–6

8 ounces fromage blanc

3 whole pimientos (hand-crushed to leave some large chunks)

1 clove garlic, smashed

¼ cup onion, minced

Salt (to taste)

Combine all ingredients in a bowl and serve on a sandwich, with crackers, or with chopped fresh vegetables.

Goat Cheese with Pepper Honey

A simple but beautifully delicious way to serve your goat cheese—in ten seconds flat!

Serves 8–10

1 (11-ounce) log goat cheese

2½ teaspoons black peppercorns, coarsely crushed

⅓ cup honey (I love Savannah Bee's Tupelo honey best)

Place goat cheese on platter. Stir pepper and honey in a measuring cup and pour over cheese. Serve with crackers or crusty French bread.

Green Apples with Chèvre and Smoked Trout

Champagne is the perfect accompaniment for this delicate appetizer.

Serves 4–6

1 unpeeled Granny Smith apple, quartered, cored, cut into ¼-inch-thick slices

2 tablespoons lemon juice, freshly squeezed

6 ounces skinless Applewood smoked trout fillets

3 ounces goat cheese, room temperature

1 small bunch watercress, thick stems trimmed

Black pepper, freshly ground, to taste

Combine apple slices and lemon juice in medium bowl; toss gently to coat. Cut trout fillets lengthwise in half, then cut each half into apple-slice-size pieces. Drain apple slices; place on platter. Spread goat cheese on each apple slice, and top with 1 watercress sprig and 1 trout piece. Sprinkle with pepper. (Can be made 2 hours ahead. Cover and chill.) Serve.

Split Pea Hummus

This fun Southern twist on traditional hummus is inexpensive and tasty. Serve it as an appetizer with fresh vegetables and pita chips.

Serves 6

1 cup dried green split peas

1 garlic clove

½ teaspoon salt, divided

¼ cup olive oil

1 tablespoon lemon juice

¼ teaspoon cumin, ground

Sort and wash peas. Bring garlic and 3 cups water to a boil in medium saucepan. Add peas; return to a boil. Cover, reduce heat, and simmer 25 minutes. Stir in ¼ teaspoon salt; cook 15 minutes or until tender. Drain. Combine peas, olive oil, lemon juice, cumin, and remaining ¼ teaspoon salt in a food processor; pulse 5–7 times or until smooth, stopping to scrape sides as needed. Serve at room temperature.

Goat Cheese Queso

Serves 6

2 tablespoons butter

½ cup onions, minced

Salt and pepper

1 tablespoon garlic, chopped

1 jalapeño, stemmed, seeded, and chopped

8 ounces goat cheese, crumbled

¼ to ½ cup heavy cream

½ cup tomato, chopped

2–3 tablespoons fresh cilantro leaves, finely chopped

Homemade or store bought tortilla chips, for serving

Melt the butter in a saucepan over medium heat. Add the onions and sauté for 2 minutes. Season with salt and pepper. Stir in garlic, jalapeño, cheese, and cream. Cook for 3–5 minutes or until thickened. Season with salt and pepper, to taste. Sprinkle tomato and cilantro over top and serve with tortilla chips.

Chive-Goat Cheese Dip with Crudités

This is an elegant appetizer that couldn't be more simple. It's best served with spring vegetables that are still tiny and tender. For kids or adults, it's a crowd pleaser.

Serves 6

1 bunch radishes, thinly sliced

1 bunch baby carrots

1 zucchini, cut into thin strips (or baby zucchini, halved, if you can find them)

1 pint yellow grape tomatoes, halved

4 ounces goat cheese

⅓ cup heavy cream

3 tablespoons chives, thinly sliced

¼ teaspoon salt

⅛ teaspoon black pepper, freshly ground

Stir the goat cheese, cream, chives, salt, and pepper in a bowl until a creamy texture is reached. Season to taste if necessary. Sometimes I add a squirt of lemon juice.

Arrange the vegetables on a tray next to the goat cheese dip. Sit back and relax.

Goat Cheese Gratin

This was one of my first favorite appetizers, which I will never, ever make without thinking about my friend Anne Cain. She loved it so much, I ended up sending her a case of our Confetti so she could make this anytime her little heart desired.

Serves 6

10 ounces Belle Chèvre Confetti

2 teaspoons fresh oregano, chopped

2 dozen Niçoise olives, pitted and halved

2 teaspoons fresh rosemary, chopped

2 cups spicy tomato sauce, Arrabiata or Arabica

Preheat broiler. Scatter goat cheese on bottom of gratin dish. Sprinkle with half of the herbs. Top with tomato sauce. Sprinkle remaining herbs and olives over top. Broil until cheese is melted and fragrant and tomato sauce is sizzling, about 8–10 minutes. Serve with toasted baguette slices.

Tapenade-Walnut Tart with Goat Cheese

This is great for parties. It's always a hit and comes together in just a couple of minutes of hands-on time. I've even had self-proclaimed olive haters gobble it up and then ask me what was on it!

6 ounces goat cheese

1 roll store-bought puff pastry

4 tablespoons olive tapenade, prepared

2 teaspoons fresh thyme, chopped

½ cup walnuts, crushed and toasted

Roll out the puff pastry into a rectangle about 8 x 12 inches. Roll up the sides slightly and prick the bottom with a fork. Cook for 10 minutes at 400 degrees on a nonstick baking sheet. Remove from oven and cool.

Spread the tapenade on the cooked pastry. Sprinkle with thyme and walnuts, and cover evenly with goat cheese.

Bake for 15–20 minutes at 400 degrees until the cheese has melted and started to brown on top.

Goat Cheese and Caramelized Onion Tart

To make these tarts, two 13½ x 4 x 1-inch tart pans with removable rims are ideal; however, you could also use one 11 x 1-inch round tart pan with a removable rim.

Alternatively, you can make these free-form, laying out the crust and folding over the edges for a rustic look and feel.

Serves 8

2¼ sticks (18 tablespoons) butter, unsalted, cold

2 cups all-purpose flour

½ teaspoon salt

2–4 tablespoons ice water

3 onions (about 1½ pounds total), thinly sliced

2 tablespoons olive oil

Pie weights or raw rice for weighting shells

10 ounces mild goat cheese (about 1 heaping cup), softened

¾ cup sour cream

3 large eggs

1 teaspoon fresh thyme leaves

To make the dough, cut 1¼ sticks butter into bits (reserve remaining butter and let soften), and

use a food processor or a bowl with a pastry blender to blend or pulse together with flour and salt until mixture resembles coarse meal. Add 2 tablespoons ice water and toss with a fork or pulse until incorporated. Add enough remaining ice water to form a dough, 1 tablespoon at a time, tossing with fork or pulsing to incorporate. On a work surface, smear dough with heel of hand in 3 or 4 forward motions to make dough easier to work with. Divide dough in half and pat each half into a rectangle, about 6 x 3 inches. Chill rectangles, wrapped separately in plastic wrap, at least 1 hour and up to 1 week.

Preheat oven to 375 degrees.

On a lightly floured surface, roll out 1 dough rectangle into a 16 x 6-inch rectangle and fit it into a 13½ x 4 x 1-inch tart pan with a removable fluted rim. Roll a rolling pin over pastry to trim it flush with top of rim, and prick bottom of shell in several places with a fork. Make 1 more tart shell in another tart pan in same manner.

Line shells with foil and fill with pie weights or raw rice. Bake shells in middle of oven for 10 minutes. Carefully remove foil and weights or rice, and bake shells until pale golden, about 5 minutes.

While shells are baking, whisk together goat cheese, reserved butter, and sour cream until smooth, and whisk in eggs until combined well. Season custard with salt and pepper.

Heat oil in large nonstick skillet over medium-high heat. Add onions. Sauté until onions are pale golden, about 5 minutes. Reduce heat to medium; sauté onions until tender and deep golden, about 15 minutes. Cool.

Spread onions evenly in shells, and pour custard over onions. Sprinkle thyme over custard and bake tarts in middle of oven for 20 minutes, or until puffed and golden. Cool tarts in pans on racks (filling will deflate). Tarts may be made 2 days ahead, cooled completely and chilled, covered, in pans. Reheat tarts in pans, uncovered, in a 350-degree oven for about 15 minutes to crisp crusts. Remove rims from pans.

Cut tarts crosswise into ¾-inch-wide slices to make about 32 hors d'oeuvres; if desired, halve slices crosswise again to make about 64 hors d'oeuvres. Serve tarts warm or at room temperature.

Oven-Roasted Red Peppers with Goat Cheese

These heavenly soft roasted peppers with creamy fillings work both as a side dish and as a main course with a salad and crusty bread. Also try with tomatoes.

Serves 12

12 medium red peppers

1⅔ pounds goat cheese

1 large egg, lightly beaten

2 cloves garlic, minced

2 tablespoons basil, finely chopped

1 teaspoon kosher salt

¼ teaspoon black pepper, freshly ground

¼ cup extra-virgin olive oil

Preheat the oven to 425 degrees. Slice off the top half-inch of each pepper and reserve the tops. Scoop out the cores and seeds. Cut a very thin sliver off the bottom of each pepper to help them stand up straight. Arrange the peppers in a 9 x 13-inch glass or ceramic baking dish.

In a bowl, combine the goat cheese with the egg, garlic, basil, salt, pepper and 2 tablespoons of the olive oil. Spoon the goat cheese mixture into the peppers, mounding the filling ½ inch above the top. Cover with the pepper tops and drizzle with the remaining 2 tablespoons of olive oil.

Bake the peppers for 35 minutes until tender and browned in spots and the cheese is hot. Let stand for 15 minutes. Serve warm or at room temperature.

Dates with Goat Cheese Wrapped in Prosciutto

Serves 8

⅓ cup goat cheese

1 tablespoon oregano

Pinch salt and pepper

16 Medjool dates, pitted

16 large basil leaves

4-inch-wide, thin slices prosciutto di Parma, each cut into 4 long strips

16 toothpicks, soaked in water 10 minutes

Set oven to broil.

Mix goat cheese with oregano, salt, and pepper. Spoon 1 teaspoon cheese into each date; wrap with a basil leaf and then a prosciutto strip. Secure with a toothpick. Broil until cheese bubbles, about 3 minutes. Serve warm.

Spiced Popcorn

I don't keep pre-made snacks around—even for the children—so this is a fun and easy one and it also dresses up well if you like for the evening. Just toss the popcorn in some truffle oil or truffle salt for a grown up flavor.

Serves 6

1 bag natural popcorn, such as Black Jewell, microwaved according to directions

2 tablespoons melted butter

½ teaspoon sweet paprika

1 teaspoon salt

½ teaspoon garlic powder

1 teaspoon cumin

¼ teaspoon cayenne pepper

Empty popped popcorn from the bag into a large serving bowl. Drizzle with melted butter. Combine spices in a small dish and sprinkle the blend over hot corn. Serve.

Goat Cheese Torta

This is always a big hit at parties!

Serves 25

10 ounces goat cheese

2 cloves garlic, chopped

½ cup pesto, or to taste

½ cup fine oil-packed sun-dried tomatoes, chopped up (including 1–2 teaspoons of the marinade)

Mix goat cheese and cream cheese; add garlic. If you want, add salt and black pepper to taste.

Line a small glass bowl (about 2–3 cups) with plastic wrap. Put about ⅓ of the goat cheese mix into the bowl. Top this with the pesto (at least ½ cup), another ¼ of the goat cheese mix, and then the sun-dried tomatoes. Top with the rest of the cheese. Cover with plastic wrap. Refrigerate for at least 2 hours and up to four days.

To serve, invert bowl on a serving dish. Carefully remove the plastic wrap.

Decorate with fresh herbs, such as branches of thyme, oregano, rosemary, and parsley. Serve with baguette slices.

Belle's Southern Pesto Spread

Serves 6

4 ounces mild goat cheese, room temperature

2 ounces cream cheese, room temperature

¼ cup pesto (see recipe on page 46)

Stir together all ingredients with salt and pepper to taste until smooth.

It's a Greek Southern Thing!

My history before I turned fifteen was mostly shaped by my Alabama horizons: the creeks, Guntersville Lake, the feel of the grasses on my bare feet, and the smells of my grandmother's lunches served on the dock. It is difficult for me to describe a meaning-ful day in my life without using the word "food," and that has a great deal to do with my Southern heritage and maternal grandmother.

But "food" for me also has a great deal to do with my Greek heritage, which I didn't come into until I was a young adult.

I traveled to Greece for the first time, at fifteen, to visit my family there. I didn't speak the language or understand intrinsically the culture I was being introduced to, but it ended up shaping me nonetheless.

The amazing thing is that these two seemingly very different cultures are, in actuality, very similar—very, very similar—especially where food and hospitality are concerned. Aren't I lucky?

Both cultures have an unspoken language that dominates the traditions of the table. I still to this day don't speak much Greek, and my Greek stepmother doesn't speak much English, but I came to understand that the language in which love is communicated to one's family is the kind that you can put on your plate. The number one reason I continue to go to Greece, aside from my beloved family, is the food. It's best served in someone's home (although the tavernas do a pretty damned good job) because Greeks have an almost fierce desire to please one's guests, not with lavish furnishings in one's home, and not with the witty and stimulating conversation (though those are always lively), but with the food.

Women in Greece, not unlike women in the South, compete for attention on who makes the best fritters or moussaka—even family members vie for the title of "the best"; I do with my two Greek sisters. The only difference I can articulate between the two cultures in this aspect has to do with articulation itself—Greeks are vividly verbal whereas a Southern lady would demurely defer her rightful title to someone else.

The Southern Recipes website (olsouthrecipes. com) has a section called "Etiquette at the Southern Table." I couldn't help smiling when I read that "much of Southern life revolves around food, and when you enter a Southerner's home, even for a casual visit, you should expect to be offered a snack and beverage." Interestingly enough, these customs could just as easily describe a dinner table in Greece.

To arrive at my grandmother's house as a child to spend a weekend or sometimes an exultant whole week was to be rewarded with treats in all the corners and cupboards in her kitchen. The freezer and pantry, the pot on the stove, and the biscuit bowl on her counter all held wonders.

I knew when a visit was due when she called and said that she was cooking up things that only I adored.

My beloved Southern grandmother is no longer living, but I discover the same joy from my stepmother every time I visit my family in Greece.

I was given a wonderful gift with both of these heritages, and it is an easy one to share. For me, cooking and feeding friends and family are, and will always be, forms of celebration, times to play.

Here are a few of my favorite Southern recipes and a few of my favorite Greek ones.

I hope you enjoy!

Fried Chicken

Every time I fry chicken I get a few knots in my stomach. A person is judged by her fried chicken in the South—but only politely so, in that quintessential silent way that words not said can be more important than words that are. I agree with Martha Foose, a Southern cook I admire, when she says, "Proper fried chicken takes a long time to master. If you want to make good fried chicken, you must make it often and learn the nuances." Well said.

Despite this simple dish's ability to intimidate me every time anew, it is still one of my all-time favorite meals. If forced to choose, I always say my two favorite foods are fried chicken and pâté.

Cook's note: Don't let having to cut up a whole chicken deter you from making this dish. Ask your butcher to do it for you or buy your favorite chicken parts.

Serves 4–6

1 (3-pounds) whole chicken, cut up

2 cups unbleached all-purpose flour

Salt and pepper

Dash cayenne pepper

2 cups peanut oil (my preference) or lard

Rinse chicken in warm water. Pat dry with paper towels.

Heat oil in cast-iron skillet on very high heat.

Combine flour, salt, pepper and dash of cayenne pepper in a bowl and mix to combine. Dredge chicken pieces in flour mixture. Set aside for a few minutes while oil comes to temperature.

Dredge chicken pieces a second time in the flour mixture.

Place chicken in the oil and fry for 8–10 minutes per side. Drain on a crumpled brown paper bag or on wire rack.

Fried chicken is good served hot, room temperature, or even cold.

Chicken and Dumplings

I called her "Grandma" though she always wanted me to call her "Grandmother." I couldn't. I was nine years old when she sprang this on me. "Grandmother?" It didn't fit. "Grandma" fit the way my favorite shirt that I insisted on wearing every day that summer fit—well and worn and familiar. (In this book, for her, in all other places I will refer to her as "Grandmother.") She remained "Grandma" and chicken and dumplings will always remain the food that conjures her memory like no other. This is not the kind of dish one just whips up in a flash; it takes a little time. It was prepared especially for me every single time I visited—without fail. And I *loved* it. It was as if Grandmother put her feelings for me inside the broth. In fact, I am certain she did, although I don't know how.

This is quite a confession I am about to make in print, but I must admit that

I do not have my grandmother's recipe and further that I have never made her chicken and dumplings and never will. I have kept a vigil in deciding never to eat this dish again—until at which point, if there is a heaven, we meet again with her pot of chicken and dumplings on the stove, simmering up just for me.

So I offer you the next best thing:

Viola Mills, a dear, dear woman, who has been at the creamery for over twenty years, is sharing hers with me so that you can enjoy it at home and make it for those that you love.

Serves 8

1 (3¾-pounds) whole chicken

½ teaspoon garlic powder

½ teaspoon dried thyme

2½ teaspoons salt, divided

¾ teaspoon black pepper, divided

1 small onion, chopped

Dumplings

⅛ teaspoon sage

⅛ onion powder

3 cups self-rising flour

⅓ cup shortening

2 teaspoons bacon drippings

1 cup milk

Bring chicken, water to cover, garlic powder, thyme, 1½ teaspoons salt, and ½ teaspoon pepper to a boil in a Dutch oven over medium heat. Cover, reduce heat to medium-low, and simmer 1 hour. Remove chicken; reserve broth.

Cool chicken 30 minutes; skin, bone, and shred chicken. Skim fat from broth. Add chicken, diced onion, and remaining 1 teaspoon salt and ¼ teaspoon

pepper to broth. Return to a simmer.

Combine flour, sage, onion powder, and generous sprinkling of salt and pepper in a bowl. Cut in shortening and bacon drippings with a pastry blender until crumbly. Stir in milk. Turn dough out onto a lightly floured surface. Roll to ⅛-inch thickness; cut into 1-inch pieces.

Drop dumplings, a few at a time, into simmering broth, stirring gently.

Cover and simmer, stirring often, 25 minutes.

Marinated Cucumbers and Onions

These were always in a bowl in my grandmother's fridge. I would just dip my greedy little fingers in the bowl and fish out the cucumbers and onions as a summer snack.

Serves 4

Marinade

4 tablespoons olive oil (although I am certain my grandmother didn't use olive oil but it is my go-to oil)

3 tablespoons apple cider vinegar

½ teaspoon kosher salt

¼ teaspoon sugar

Cracked black pepper

Salad

1 large cucumber peeled, sliced into ¼-inch rounds

1 medium sweet onion, cut in half and thinly sliced

In a small mixing bowl combine all marinade ingredients, whisking until well blended.

Gently toss vegetables in the marinade and let them soak for at least 30 minutes or overnight in refrigerator.

Serve as a side to a sandwich or on a lunch buffet.

Buttermilk Cornbread

This is a recipe that I have memorized, one that has been stuck in my head for the longest time, maybe it is even in my blood. It is your basic but brilliant cornbread recipe. You can snazz it up if you care to with chopped onions, or jalapeños, or even cheese, but I prefer it just plain for eating with chili and soups of all kinds or just on its own with lots of hot melted butter dripping off the side.

You have heard it a million times I am sure but it is worth repeating: Nothing beats a good seasoned cast-iron skillet for your cornbread. To get the crispy crust—the best part of the cornbread if you ask me, like the icing on a cake—make sure to thoroughly pre-heat the skillet before pouring in the batter.

Cook's note: Use leftover cornbread to make large

croutons for soups and salads. Cube the bread and brush with melted butter then toast them up nicely in the oven. They are delicious!

Serves 6

1 egg, beaten

2 cups buttermilk

1¾ stone-ground cornmeal

2 teaspoons bacon grease, strained

1 teaspoon baking powder

1 teaspoon baking soda

1 teaspoon salt

Pour the bacon grease in the skillet and swirl to coat the bottom and sides. Put the skillet into a cold oven and preheat to 450 degrees, warming the pan at the same time the oven comes to temperature.

In a mixing bowl combine the buttermilk and egg well. Add the cornmeal and beat it into the batter. Add baking powder, soda, and salt and mix in well.

Remove skillet from oven and pour batter into hot skillet.

Return to oven and bake for 20 minutes or until the top is nice and brown.

Turn the bread out onto a plate and serve with butter.

Cheeseburger in Paradise

On my first trip to Greece to spend a summer with my Greek family, my fifteen-year-old self did not make friends with the food. I thought that they had it all wrong.

My Greek stepmother is a Greek goddess sent to earth in mortal form to make sure her brood's every need is met—but not in a June Cleaver kind of way, as she is just as fiery as any Greek. She tried so hard to please my fickle teenage-American sensibilities with her cooking.

Thinking Americans like eggs and bacon for breakfast, that is what I got, but it was not bacon by my assessment, and the eggs were scrambled all wrong and brown and with the bacon cooked in it.

And it wasn't just the eggs and bacon that were twisted.

Three weeks into that first trip I thought I might die if I couldn't have something familiar to eat. My father noted my discontent and told me that if I could just hold on until later in the week we would go to a place, a special place, a few towns over that made a fantastic cheeseburger. He was going well out of his way to please me and I knew it and I also knew that it must indeed be a great place, one schooled in the ways of American fare, as he, true to fashion, had built it up in my mind as the *best* (a phrase that I now realize accompanied anything that *he* liked).

Over the next few days, I had dreams of that cheeseburger like a teenage boy might dream of, well, whatever it is that teenage boys dream of.

The day finally came. I remember walking up to the restaurant—a small bar-like place that had a counter where you could order and just a few small tables inside spilling out to more on the sidewalk. The sign outside had the comforting and familiar red and white of my Coca-Cola South, a sign that meant to me at that moment that we had come to the right place.

Alas, when the cheeseburger was delivered there was no familiar orangey cheese melting and spilling outside its bun borders. Yet the fries that I ordered were spilling out! Fries on the burger??!! There were onions, but they were cooked inside the patty (just like the bacon all mingled inside the eggs).

My heart had already sunk just looking at it after it was delivered. It was not a cheeseburger, and to my limited and very shallow fifteen-year-old-self I was not in paradise.

Hushpuppies

There were always hushpuppies at my grandmother's fish fries every summer, and for me they were the highlight of the entire affair. I could have eaten them like popcorn! I still love them so.

Serves 8

Buttermilk Cornbread (see recipe on page 69)

½ cup onion, chopped

⅓ cup unbleached all-purpose flour

Corn oil for frying

Heat oil in deep-fat fryer to 365 degrees. Drop batter by tablespoonfuls into oil and fry until golden brown, roughly 3 minutes.

Greek Meatballs

The Greeks do beginnings very, very well. Mezes are small plates that are brought before a meal, and you can fill a whole table with the selections that are available there.

A small rough place in Preveza, Greece, did them the best. It was a place made colorful by the shouts, hands, and weathered faces of fishermen and other laborers who populated it. Mezes and ouzo were in abundance.

For the ground beef, I sometimes use a mixture of pork and beef, for a very nice result.

My favorite addition to the meatballs is tzatziki, a classic Greek dipping sauce that is served with pita or grilled meats (see recipe following). I now make mine with a little goat cheese, which makes it a bit thicker. I could eat it with a spoon!

Serves 6

Greek Meatballs

1 pound ground beef

1 egg

¼ cup dried breadcrumbs

¼ cup fresh mint, chopped

¼ cup green onions, chopped

1 small garlic clove, finely diced

¼ teaspoon kosher salt

Preheat oven to 475 degrees. In a bowl, combine all ingredients without overmixing; I use my hands. Season with salt and pepper.

Cook's note: If you like, you can place a tiny ball-shaped piece of meat in a hot skillet to test for correct seasoning.

Form 1½-inch balls from the mixture. Place balls on a wire rack set on top of a baking sheet. (These are more traditional if fried in olive oil on the stove top, but I find that the oven at high heat gives a great

if you don't drain them they will make your tzatziki runny.)

When cucumbers are done draining, combine all ingredients in a food processor. Pulse until well blended and there are no oversized cucumber pieces in the mix.

Best if made a couple of hours ahead of time so that flavors can steep. Use leftovers as a sandwich spread.

Saganaki

Saganaki dishes take their name from the pan in which they are made. A sagani is a two-handled pan that is made in many different styles. In the market, look for a small paella pan, cast-iron skillet, or even an oval au gratin dish.

Serve this as an appetizer or part of a larger selection of mezes—small plates. The key to success with this dish is to get the oil hot before frying so it doesn't smoke.

Serves 6

1 pound cheese, kefalotyri or kasseri (or substitute Pecorino Romano)

½ cup olive oil

⅔ cup all-purpose flour

2–3 lemons, quartered

Cut the cheese into slices or wedges that are ½-inch thick and 2½- to 3-inches wide. Moisten each slice with cold water and dredge in the flour. In a sagani (Greek pan used for this dish) or a small, heavy-bottomed frying pan (cast-iron works best), heat the oil over medium-high heat, and sear each slice in 1 tablespoon of oil until golden-brown on both sides. Serve hot with a last-minute squeeze of fresh lemon juice.

Add ouzo or wine, olives, vegetable mezes, tomatoes, and crusty bread.

crispy texture and saves the messy frying.)

Cook in oven for 10–12 minutes or until done.

Tzatziki

Serves 8

6 ounces Greek yogurt, strained

2 ounces goat cheese

½ cup English cucumber, peeled, seeded, and diced

¼ cup lemon juice, freshly squeezed

2 tablespoons fresh dill

1 garlic clove

¼ teaspoon salt

Salt cucumbers and let drain in a colander. (It is amazing how much water the cucumbers will give off, and

Greek Zucchini Fritters— Kolokithokeftedes

A fritter, by definition, is typically made with a batter producing a light and fluffy interior, usually with the aid of baking soda and powder. This recipe is really more a cake or pattie.

In Greece it is typical to have these as part of mezes, but they could very easily be served as a vegetable side dish.

Serves 6

2 medium or large zucchini, coarsely grated

3 tablespoons fresh mint, finely chopped

2 tablespoons fresh dill, finely chopped

½ cup feta cheese, crumbled

4 green onions including green parts, chopped

1 large egg

½ cup all-purpose flour

4 tablespoons Panko breadcrumbs

Sea or kosher salt

Olive oil

Wash zucchini. Leaving skins on, grate them with the coarse side of a grater. Put the grated zucchini in a colander and sprinkle liberally with salt. Let sit and drain for at least 30 minutes while you prepare the other ingredients.

Remove the zucchini by the handful, squeezing to remove as much liquid as you can. Put it in a bowl with herbs, feta, and green onions. Mix with a fork. Add a lightly beaten egg and stir. Add flour and breadcrumbs. The mixture should be wet but not watery. Mix in salt to taste.

Heat olive oil in a pan about ⅛-inch deep covering the entire pan. When hot, scoop out spoonfuls of the zucchini mixture and put them in the pan. Let them cook about 3–4 minutes or until brown, and then flip them. Cook another 3–4 minutes until browned. Remove fritters and place on a paper towel-lined plate to remove excess oil.

Serve hot with tzatziki (see recipe on page 73).

Greek Salad

One summer after returning from Greece I was so filled with adoration for the simplicity of the Greek salad, I ate it for almost every meal for an entire month. And, yes, finally it happened—I needed a break from my beloved.

I have never met a Greek salad in Greece that was served with lettuce. Traditionally, the salad is only vegetables topped with a generous slice of feta. Part of the beauty of this salad is when it contains the freshest possible tomatoes. I believe that (as my father would say) you can only get the *best* tomatoes direct from the soil of an Alabama or Greek summer.

Serves 2

1 beautiful vine ripe tomato

½ large English cucumber, peeled

½ red onion, cut in 4 pieces

4 ounces cut of good quality feta (blasphemy, I know, but I love the French feta—and honestly so do a lot of Greeks)

½ cup olive oil

2½ tablespoons red wine vinegar

½ teaspoon dried oregano

Salt and pepper

Combine all ingredients except feta and toss to combine. (I don't emulsify the dressing; just drizzle on top and then toss—simple and good!)

Put in a pretty bowl, and top with the feta chunk. Add a little extra oregano if you like.

Moussaka

I need to let you know right off the bat that moussaka is not a recipe, it's an event. Almost a full day event. And preferably an event that you can share with a few close friends in the kitchen to help you get through it cheerfully. I love making this dish best when my sisters are visiting. Actually, we all take turns making it, chiding and bragging that ours is the best, all the while fending off advice from the other two and swatting away menacing hands reaching for the best slices of eggplant.

On second thought, maybe it is best to do it in a kitchen free of distractions!

Tastes even better the next day.

Serves 6

Eggplant
2 large eggplants (about 2¾ pounds), unpeeled and cut lengthwise into ½-inch slices

½ cup extra-virgin olive oil

Kosher salt and pepper

Meat Sauce
2 tablespoons extra-virgin olive oil

½ medium yellow onion, chopped

3 cloves garlic, minced

1 pound ground beef

½ teaspoon dried oregano

⅛ teaspoon allspice, ground

2 whole cloves (remove from sauce before final assembly)

1 teaspoon cinnamon

½ teaspoon kosher salt, plus to taste

Black pepper, freshly ground

1½ cups canned tomatoes, whole, peeled, roughly chopped

Bay leaf

Béchamel
5 tablespoons butter, unsalted

6 tablespoons all-purpose flour

3 cups whole milk, room temperature

1½ teaspoons kosher salt

¼ teaspoon nutmeg

1 large egg

2 large egg yolks

3 tablespoons Gruyère, grated

Salt the eggplant, and slice into half-inch slices. Place the eggplant slices in a colander and salt them liberally. (The salt helps to remove some of the bitterness of the eggplant.) Cover them with an inverted plate, weighed down with a heavy can or jar. Place the colander in the sink so that excess moisture can be drawn out. They will need to sit for at least 15–20 minutes, preferably an hour.

Heat a skillet or griddle. Sauté the eggplant in olive oil until soft, but they are best when their edges are a little crispy. Set aside, covered.

To make the meat sauce, heat the olive oil in a large skillet over medium-high heat. Add the onion and cook, stirring with a wooden spoon, until lightly browned, about 4 minutes. Add the garlic and cook, stirring frequently, until fragrant, about 1 minute. Add beef, oregano, allspice, cloves, and cinnamon. Break the meat up into small pieces, and season with the ½ teaspoon salt and pepper, to taste. Cook, stirring occasionally, for about 2 minutes. Lower the heat to medium and cook, stirring, until just cooked but still slightly pink inside, about 1 minute. Add the tomatoes and bay leaf and bring to a simmer. Cook until the sauce is thickened and fragrant, about 20 minutes.

For the béchamel, melt the butter in a medium saucepan over medium heat. Whisk in the flour until smooth. Cook, stirring, for 1 minute. Remove pan from heat and add milk, salt, and nutmeg. Return to the heat and, whisking constantly, bring to a boil. Simmer 2 minutes. Transfer the sauce to a bowl and stir to cool. When the sauce is cool, whisk in the egg and yolks.

Assemble the moussaka. Lower the oven to 350 degrees. Lay half of the eggplant in the pan, overlapping the slices if needed. Cover with half of the meat sauce and smooth with a rubber spatula. Repeat with the remaining eggplant and meat sauce. Pour the béchamel over the layered mixture and smooth with a rubber spatula. Sprinkle with the Gruyère and bake, uncovered, until lightly browned and the custard is set, about 1 hour.

Remove the moussaka from the oven and let rest for 10 minutes. Use a slotted spoon or spatula to serve.

Main Courses
What Are We Playing Tonight?

Some rules are hard to break. Growing up, my dinner plate always looked pretty much the same and my mother would explain it to me like this: "You have to have a meat, a starch, and a vegetable." I am not sure I knew what a starch was but I knew it wasn't a real dinner unless we had one on our plate.

Even though I have long since left that school of thought about supper (or dinner, depending on where you are from), the ghost of that hard and fast rule still haunts me. If I want to make a salad as a main course I find myself thinking it has to include a protein or starch. Or when I go to prepare even the simplest of meals for just myself and my son, I find that the strict formula is still in the back of my head.

I believe routines are good and healthy and they certainly make life easier when it comes to getting food prepared when we are in a hurry. There are a million and one books out there that will give Americans simple rules to follow for getting a work week organized—everything from packing lunches the night before, to laying out one's clothes, to making a weeks' worth of meals on a Sunday night.

You won't find me providing any such formula or advice. The kitchen is a playground and should be approached that way—with a smile on our faces. Somehow we have let stress enter our kitchens, either about how quickly we have to get dinner on the table, what in the world we might prepare, or "you invited *who* over tonight?!"

Earlier this year I came home to a rather bare refrigerator and pantry but thought I can certainly do *something* with this cabbage, green onion, and chicken breast. I put the question out to my friends on Facebook: "What would you make for supper with only these three ingredients?"

I ended up getting a ton of great ideas (although a few friends told me to scrap it all and order take-out!). It was a fun exercise for which the point is that our normal formulas or old standbys don't have to come into the mix if we approach the kitchen with a willingness to play and a little creativity.

Have fun!

Iced Green Tea

For the longest time my son didn't know there was any other tea besides green tea. I was sort of embarrassed even when a neighbor gave me a sideways glance after asking him if he wanted something to drink and he replied, "green tea, please."

I grew up with regular black tea, the Southern staple, so oversweetened that now I can hardly stand any sugar in my tea. This recipe calls for Splenda, or you can simply sweeten to your desired taste.

I find green tea exceptionally refreshing and the health benefits are an added bonus.

Serves 4

4 cups boiling water

8 green tea bags

2 cups cold water

½ cup Splenda (no-calorie artificial sweetener)

In a saucepan, pour boiling water over tea bags; cover and steep 5 minutes. Remove tea bags from water, squeezing gently. Stir in 2 cups cold water and sweetener, stirring until sweetener dissolves. Serve over ice or let tea come to room temperature and then serve over ice.

Adalene's Famous Mint Iced Tea

Adalene Kelly Bledsoe, my son Kelly's paternal grandmother, is known for many things, including her Southern charm, incredible generosity, and iced tea. The latter is delicious and served up with a smile every time you visit. It has graced humble picnic tables (always transported in recycled gallon jars that had once housed giant pickles, acquired in bulk, so she could make and then gift her delicious garlic pickles at Christmas), held together countless garden club meetings, and always served at parties for those too young or faint of heart for the scotch and soda.

3 family-size tea bags (I use Lipton's)

4 lemons squeezed

2 cups sugar (or to taste)

Handful of fresh mint (approximately ½ cup crushed)

Steep tea in a tea pot (china preferred) 10–15 minutes (or less, to desired strength). In a gallon pitcher (pottery or glass), place the sugar, mint, and the lemon juice (with the lemon rinds). Pour the hot steeped tea in the pitcher and allow the mixture to cool. Fill the pitcher with cold water, strain, and serve over ice. You may add a sprig of fresh mint to the top of the glass for garnish. Makes a gallon.

Stuffed Tomatoes

I hated stuffed tomatoes and stuffed peppers growing up. My mom, who only cooked occasionally, would frequently make them. How this dish was reinvented for me later in Greece—what did these two cultures have to do with one another anyway?—I will never know. I soon found myself friends with this dish in a way that surprised me especially as my two disparate cultures have them in common.

Gemista is the Greek name for stuffed tomatoes and it is one of the most popular vegetarian dishes in the summer.

Although the common English translation of *gemista* is stuffed tomatoes, in Greece this particular recipe involves much more than tomatoes. *Gemista* are actually made of stuffed tomatoes, stuffed bell peppers and sometimes zucchini, eggplants or even stuffed potatoes.

Feel free to try this recipe in other vegetables besides the tomato.

Serves 6

12 firm, ripe tomatoes

Kosher salt

Sugar

3 tablespoons olive oil

1 medium onion, finely chopped

2 cloves garlic, chopped

¼ cup fresh parsley, chopped

½ pound lean ground lamb or beef if you cannot find the lamb

¼ cup dry white wine

¼ cup water

6 tablespoons raw white rice, long-grain

Black pepper, freshly ground

2 sprigs fresh mint

Preheat oven to 350 degrees. Wash the tomatoes, then turn each stem-side down, and with a sharp knife carefully cut the end to make the "lid." Remove but do not discard as you will top the tomato before baking. With a small spoon, carefully scoop the pulp into a bowl so you don't break the outer skin of the tomatoes. Set aside. Place the tomato shells in a baking-serving dish large enough to support them touching. Sprinkle

the inside of the shells with salt and sugar.

Meanwhile, prepare the stuffing. Heat the oil in a heavy skillet and add the onions. Cook over moderate heat until soft and transparent, then add the garlic and parsley, and blend. Add the meat, mashing with a fork, then add the wine and water, cover, and simmer for a few minutes. Add the rice and tomato pulp and stir. (Water or additional tomato juice from the pulp may be added if necessary, if the mixture doesn't provide enough liquid for the rice to absorb.) Cover the skillet and simmer about 7 minutes, then add salt, pepper, and mint. Taste for seasoning. Remove from heat, and fill the tomatoes up about two-thirds of the way with the stuffing and liquid. Cover with tomato lids, brush with oil.

Bake until the rice is tender (approximately 50 minutes to 1 hour), basting inside the tomatoes with the liquid released by them. Serve warm.

Rosemary and Lemon Roasted Chicken

Taste of the South magazine published this recipe of mine this year in a lovely feature on my Sunday Suppers. It was an honor to be included in their publication.

Serves 4

2 tablespoons extra-virgin olive oil

4 tablespoons fresh rosemary, chopped

2 teaspoons dried oregano

5 cloves garlic, minced

2 teaspoons lemon zest

1 (7-pound) whole chicken, giblets removed, rinsed and patted dry

Dinner Drinks

When my son was four years old his honorary Aunt Terri came to visit for a weekend from Atlanta. One of the first lessons she taught him, even as she was still not quite fully inside the door, was about the most important question a host can ask their incoming guest. "Kelly," she spoke animatedly, as an adult tends to do with young children, "what is the first thing you should say when someone comes to visit?" Blank stare in return. "May I offer you a cocktail, please?"

Kelly went around for weeks offering up that question to everyone he met, much to my chagrin and to Terri's delight.

Despite the amusing absurdity, which Terri and I both adored, of a four-year-old boy offering a cocktail, it does hold a little water in the South. Even if you are visiting a teetotaler's household, the same phrase will be uttered substituting the word "cocktail" for the word "drink"—the drink being, undoubtedly, sweet tea (see recipe for Adalene's Mint Iced Tea on page 80).

There are two main drinks you are apt to be served upon your arrival at my house for dinner: mint juleps or champagne.

Mint Juleps

There are a lot of Southern cocktails but none so lovely as the mint julep.

Always made with fresh mint, good bourbon, and plenty of crushed or shaved ice, it is the official drink of the Kentucky Derby. Traditionally, mint juleps are served in silver or pewter cups that allow for a wonderful frost to form on the outside of the cup.

When to actually add mint leaves into the Julep drink always stirs debate. Arguments rage over its proper usage, some voting for muddling the leaves with water and sugar, others for infusing them in the syrup, and a third faction maintaining that a sprig as garnish should suffice.

I like to muddle the mint with a mortar and pestle, making my simple syrup separately. I don't like them very sweet so I offer the syrup on the side in a tiny little pitcher for guests to add to taste.

For Each Serving:

Handful of mint leaves

Crushed ice

Simple syrup (see recipe below)

2 ounces good-quality Kentucky bourbon

Crush or muddle the few mint leaves in a mortar and pestle until a paste forms.

Fill the mint julep cups half full with crushed or shaved ice. Add prepared mint syrup and bourbon. Stir until the silver cup is frosted on the outside.

Simple Syrup

1 cup sugar

1 cup water

In a medium saucepan, combine sugar and water. Boil for 5 minutes, without stirring. Cool. Can be stored in refrigerator for 1 week.

Dinner drinks continued on page 85. MAIN COURSES 83

¼ teaspoon black pepper, freshly ground

Lemon juice (optional)

Bring a pot of salted water to a boil and add pasta.

Meanwhile, heat olive oil in a 10-inch skillet over high heat until just beginning to smoke, and add mushrooms. Allow to cook without moving for a minute or two. Then stir and add shallot (with salt and pepper), sautéing until tender.

Drain pasta (reserving cooking water if not using chicken jus). Toss with goat cheese and mushrooms, adding chicken stock until cheese coats hot noodles. Season to taste. Add a squeeze of lemon juice to taste.

Goat Cheese Ravioli with Three Peppers

Serves 4

Bell Peppers

2 small red bell peppers

2 small yellow bell peppers

1 small green bell pepper

2 tablespoons olive oil

½ cup onion, chopped

½ cup tomatoes, seeded and diced

2 teaspoons red wine vinegar

Ravioli

Cornmeal for sprinkling

8 ounces goat cheese

⅓ cup Parmesan, grated, plus additional for sprinkling

¼ cup mascarpone

2 tablespoons assorted fresh herbs,
(such as basil, chives, mint, and tarragon), chopped

18 wonton wrappers

4 tablespoons (½ stick) butter

¼ cup pine nuts, toasted

¼ cup Niçoise olives, pitted, thinly sliced

¼ cup fresh chives, chopped

Char all peppers over gas flame or in broiler until blackened on all sides. Place in paper bag; seal and let stand at room temperature 15 minutes. Peel and seed peppers; chop.

Heat oil in large skillet over medium heat. Add onion and tomatoes and cook until onion begins to brown, about 4 minutes. Reduce heat to low; cook until vegetables are very soft and onion is brown, stirring often, about 15 minutes. Add chopped peppers and vinegar. Season with salt and pepper.

Cook's note: Can be made 1 day ahead. Cover; chill.

For ravioli, lightly sprinkle rimmed baking sheet with cornmeal. Mix goat cheese, Parmesan, and mascarpone with assorted fresh herbs in medium bowl. Arrange 6 wonton wrappers on work surface. Place 1 tablespoon cheese filling in center of each wrapper. Using fingertip, dampen edges of wrappers with water. Fold all 4 corners up to meet in center, forming pyramid shape; seal all 4 edges tightly. Pinch top to seal. Place on prepared baking sheet. Repeat with remaining wrappers and filling.

Cook's note: Can be made 8 hours ahead. Cover and chill.

Cook butter in large skillet over medium heat until beginning to brown, stirring occasionally, about 4 minutes.

Cook ravioli in pot of gently boiling salted water until tender, about 4 minutes. Transfer ravioli to skillet with browned butter. Toss over medium heat.

Meanwhile . . .

Rewarm bell pepper mixture; divide among 6 plates. Using slotted spoon, top peppers on each plate with 3 ravioli. Drizzle with any remaining browned butter. Sprinkle with Parmesan, toasted pine nuts, olives, and chives.

Orecchiette with Caramelized Onions, Sugar Snap Peas, Ricotta, and Goat Cheese

Serves 2

2 tablespoons extra-virgin olive oil

4 cups (packed) onions, chopped

1 8-ounce package trimmed sugar snap peas, cut into ½-inch pieces

1 8-ounce package orecchiette or pasta shells

½ cup whole-milk ricotta

4 ounces goat cheese, crumbled

¼ cup fresh basil leaves, torn

1½ teaspoons lemon peel, finely grated

Heat oil in large nonstick skillet over medium-high heat. Add onions. Sauté until onions are pale golden, about 5 minutes. Reduce heat to medium; sauté onions until tender and deep golden, about 15 minutes longer. Transfer ¾ cup sautéed onions to a small bowl. Add peas to onions in skillet. Sauté until peas are crisp-tender, about 3 minutes. Remove skillet from heat.

Cook pasta in large pot of boiling salted water until just tender but still firm to bite. Drain pasta, reserving 1 cup cooking liquid.

Add pasta and ½ cup cooking liquid to onion mixture; stir over medium-high heat 30 seconds. Mix in ricotta, goat cheese, basil, and lemon peel, adding more cooking liquid to moisten as needed. Season with salt and pepper.

Pasta with Grape Tomatoes and Goat Cheese

Serves 4–6

1 pound penne

2¾ pounds cherry tomatoes, halved

Chicken and Goat Cheese Enchiladas with Red Sauce

I had the pleasure of talking goat cheese on Martha Stewart Living Radio's *Living Today* show. Host Mario Bosquez was truly amazing . . . welcoming, funny, and knowledgeable.

I presented a few recipes, goat cheese with a south-of-the-border twist. They are absolutely delicious.

Serves 4

⅓ cup plus 4 tablespoons vegetable oil

10 green serrano peppers

2 medium onions, chopped

2 cloves garlic, chopped

¼ cup water

1 28-ounce can whole tomatoes

¼ cup fresh cilantro, chopped

1 teaspoon cumin

Salt and pepper, to taste

12 6-inch corn tortillas

3 poblano peppers, seeded and cut into strips

3 cups (about) chicken, cooked and shredded

1¼ pounds goat cheese

Sour cream (optional)

5–6 ounces mild goat cheese, crumbled

⅔ cup Kalamata or other brine-cured black olives, coarsely chopped

¾ cup fresh basil leaves, torn

Salt and pepper, to taste

Cook pasta in a 6-quart pot of boiling salted water until just tender, then drain.

While pasta is cooking, toss tomatoes with salt to taste in a bowl and let juices exude.

Toss hot pasta with goat cheese in a large bowl until cheese is melted and coats pasta. Add tomatoes with juices, olives, basil, and salt and pepper to taste and toss to combine.

Heat 3 tablespoons of vegetable oil over medium-high heat, and add the serrano peppers, turning occasionally for about 4 minutes. Add half of the onions and the chopped garlic and stir occasionally for 2–3 minutes. Blend hot ingredients as well as water, canned tomatoes, cilantro, cumin, and salt and pepper to taste in a food processor.

Heat ⅓ cup vegetable oil in heavy small skillet over medium-high heat. Using tongs, add 1 tortilla

Betty's Demise and the Cost of Fresh Eggs

When I was pregnant with my son I wanted more than anything to have my own hens so that I could have fresh eggs. I had always longed for fresh eggs ever since I was a child. I don't specifically recall this memory, but I'm told that this is what I told anyone who would listen. I certainly did tell my husband. Especially my husband. We had just built a house in the country—on eighty acres of land, for goodness' sake—with plenty of room for a chicken coop. He refused, claiming that it would end up, the passion, being abandoned and left for him to tend to.

I was determined. If David wouldn't help me then I would look elsewhere. I was so adamant about this desire I entreated Danny, our farm-hand at the time, to help me build a chicken coop. He refused, too, arguing that he was attacked as a child by a rooster and was deathly afraid of them.

Eight months into my pregnancy, I found a pre-built chicken coop that I could order online and have shipped to me—it was named the Chicken Condo. With minimal assembly and a little reluctant help from Danny I had my chicken coop. And because I was in a hurry—I was nesting, in a peculiar way, mind you, and didn't have much time—I purchased three laying hens, already producing eggs, as opposed to getting chicks, as is customary.

I named them. Betty, Wilma, and Aunt Eugenia. I was already a proud mother even before my son was born as I tucked my three hens into their new condo for the night.

I tended to them faithfully, intent on proving David wrong by being responsible for their well-being and not leaving him with the chore of their feeding and such. I was a good mother to my hens.

But as luck or fate or both would have it, my true motherhood came very, very quickly on the heels of the hens' arrival. My son was born at home, and on that very same day, Betty flew the coop.

Betty flew the coop as David was trying to feed and water the chickens that he had hoped he would never ever have to feed and water.

For the remainder of the day, congratulations were offered to the proud new parents with punctuated remarks of "did you know one of your chickens is out?!"

Some relatives and friends went so far, in their good-natured aims to help, as to try to catch Betty and re-deposit her back safely where she belonged—with her other two inmates.

Suffice it to say that Betty did not live long after the conclusion was reached that she would never be caught alive if David got his hands on her. He did get his hands on her and brought her in to be cooked.

We ate Betty that night. And she was good.

and cook until softened, turning once, about 15 seconds for each side. Transfer tortilla to paper towels and drain well. Repeat with remaining tortillas.

Heat remaining 1 tablespoon vegetable oil in heavy large skillet. Add remaining half of onions and poblano pepper and cook until tender, about 5 minutes. Season to taste with salt and pepper.

Lightly oil 13 x 9 x 2-inch glass baking dish. Spoon ½ cup sauce into dish. Place scant ¼ cup chicken in center of 1 tortilla. Sprinkle with 1 generous tablespoon onion mixture. Set aside ½ cup cheese for topping. Sprinkle 2 generous tablespoons cheese atop chicken. Roll up tortilla and place seam-side down in prepared dish. Repeat with remaining tortillas, chicken, onion mixture and cheese. Pour remaining sauce over enchiladas. Sprinkle with remaining cheese. Cover with foil. (Can be made 1 day ahead. Chill.)

Preheat oven to 350 degrees. Bake enchiladas, covered, until sauce bubbles and cheese melts, about 35 minutes. Serve hot with sour cream.

Goat Cheese and Asparagus Pizza

Serves 4

6 asparagus spears, trimmed, halved lengthwise, cut into 1½-inch pieces

4 ounces Belle Chèvre Tuscan Chèvre, including sun-dried tomatoes and 3 tablespoons extra-virgin olive oil from jar

1 store-bought pizza crust

3 tablespoons fresh marjoram, chopped

¼ teaspoon red pepper flakes

Preheat oven to 400 degrees. Toss asparagus with oil in medium bowl to coat. Spoon sun-dried tomatoes over pizza crust, leaving ¾-inch plain border. Scatter

asparagus with oil over tomatoes. Bake pizza 7 minutes. Remove from oven. Crumble goat cheese over pizza. Sprinkle with marjoram and red pepper flakes. Bake another 9 minutes until crust is golden around edges.

Chicken Breasts Stuffed with Herbs and Goat Cheese

Serves 4

3 whole cloves garlic, from one roasted garlic head, the rest reserved for another use

4 ounces goat cheese, softened

3 tablespoons fresh basil, thinly sliced and divided

1 tablespoon garlic, minced

4 (6-ounce) skinless, boneless chicken breast halves

1 (25½-ounce) jar Italian herb pasta sauce

8 ounces pasta

Roast garlic. Preheat the oven to 400 degrees. Peel away the outer layers of the garlic bulb skin, leaving the skins of the individual cloves intact. Using a knife, cut off ¼- to ½-inch of the top of cloves, exposing the individual cloves of garlic. Drizzle a couple teaspoons of olive oil over the garlic head, using your fingers to make sure the garlic head is well coated. Cover with aluminum foil. Bake at 400 degrees for 30–35 minutes, or until the cloves feel soft when pressed.

Combine goat cheese, 2 tablespoons basil, and minced garlic.

Cut a slit in each chicken breast, and gently insert the cheese mixture evenly among breasts. Sear chicken for 3 minutes on each side in a hot skillet. Add the pasta sauce (carefully as the skillet is hot and might cause the sauce to pop) and whole garlic cloves in the large skillet reducing heat to medium heat. Cover and cook 15 minutes or until chicken is done. Serve over prepared pasta. Garnish with 1 tablespoon basil.

Rosemary Roast Lamb

Southern Living magazine covered an Easter at my house in Alabama recently in which this dish was featured. Easter is one of those times in the year that completely define for me the alchemy of food as celebration. And it would never be complete without roast lamb.

The Greek Easter is one of the biggest celebrations of the year—the most sacred of the Greek Orthodox faith—trumping Christmas. Festivities are held all throughout Holy Week, but they build to a crescendo starting with midnight service at church, the first minutes of Easter Sunday, the Resurrection that inevitably spills out into the streets, candles being lit and exclamations of "Christo Anesti!"—"Christ is risen!"

At dawn on Easter Sunday the pits are prepared for the whole roast lamb, representing the lamb of God. My family never prepared a spit with a whole lamb, but the roasted leg of lamb done in my stepmother's modern oven was divine enough for me.

By the way, "Tasia" means "Resurrection," and Easter is my name day in Greece. Just another reason for me to love roast lamb—as if I needed an excuse!

Serves 6–8

¼ cup olive oil

2½ tablespoons fresh rosemary, chopped

6 cloves garlic, minced

1 tablespoon anchovy paste

1 teaspoon lemon zest

1 tablespoon lemon juice

1 (5–6-pound) bone-in leg of lamb

2 teaspoons salt

¾ teaspoon pepper

Combine first 6 ingredients in a small bowl.

Pat lamb dry, and place, fat side up, on a rack in a roasting pan. Make several 1-inch-deep slits in lamb with a paring knife; rub olive oil mixture over lamb, pressing mixture into slits. Cover loosely with foil, and let stand at room temperature 30 minutes.

Meanwhile, preheat oven to 400 degrees. Uncover lamb, and sprinkle with salt and pepper.

Bake at 400 degrees for 2 hours and 30 minutes or until a meat thermometer inserted into thickest portion registers 145 degrees (medium rare). Let stand 30 minutes before slicing.

Bacon and Goat Cheese-Stuffed Pork Tenderloin with Apple Chutney

Serves 4

1½–2 pounds pork tenderloin, fat and sinew removed

3 slices bacon

4 ounces Belle Chèvre Confetti

¼ cup flat-leaf parsley, coarsely chopped

1 tablespoon extra-virgin olive oil

Black pepper, freshly ground, to taste

4 8-inch lengths of kitchen twine

Apple Chutney

1 small red onion, minced

1 tablespoon butter, unsalted

1 small Fuji apple, minced

1 tablespoon lemon juice

1 tablespoon honey

1 tablespoon rice wine vinegar

Preheat the oven to 450 degrees and line a broiler pan with foil.

Fry the bacon in a large skillet, reserving the pan when done. Pat the bacon dry with paper towels and chop.

Butterfly the pork tenderloin lengthwise, slicing it down the center, but not all the way through. Open it up, and cover it with a sheet of plastic wrap. Pound it evenly with a kitchen mallet or heavy-bottomed saucepan.

Remove the plastic wrap and sprinkle the inside evenly with the bacon, goat cheese, and flat-leaf parsley. Close the tenderloin back up and tie in four evenly-spaced places with kitchen twine to keep it shut. Coat with olive oil and sprinkle with pepper.

Brown the tenderloin in the pan used for frying bacon. When all sides are brown, place it on the broiler pan and bake it in the oven for 20–30 minutes, or until a meat thermometer registers 165 degrees.

While the pork is cooking, make the chutney. Using the same skillet used for bacon and browning the tenderloin, cook the onion with the butter on medium-high heat. After about five minutes, add the minced apple, cooking for another five minutes, stirring occasionally. When the apple and onion are soft, turn the heat up and add 1 tablespoon each of lemon juice, honey, and rice wine vinegar. Stir on high for five minutes. The mixture should turn golden brown. Reduce heat to low and simmer.

When the tenderloin is done, slice it into medallions and arrange on a plate. Top with spoonfuls of the chutney, and put the remainder into a bowl for the table.

Grilled Steaks with Chèvre Compound "Butter"

The garlicky herb "butter" is similar to the butter served with escargots in southwestern France. But instead of butter we are using goat cheese for better flavor and better health!

For the Parsley-Garlic Butter, mix together in small bowl, then cover and chill:

Serves 2

8 ounces goat cheese, softened

1 tablespoon fresh parsley, finely chopped

1 tablespoon fresh chives, chopped

Garlic clove, minced

2 teaspoons Cognac

Salt and pepper

Prepare barbecue (medium-high heat). Rub with generous amounts of salt and pepper:

2 1½-inch-thick rib-eye steaks (about 1 pound each)

Grill steaks to desired doneness, about 6 minutes per side for medium-rare. Cut each steak in half, top with spoonful of chilled butter, and serve.

Savory Cakes, Some of My Favorite Things

I was such a tomboy. Which means, of course, that I loved to play in the dirt. In fact, I still like to play in the dirt and am so glad I have a son who likes to play in the creek like I did. It wasn't that long ago that I got to teach Kelly how to find underneath the rocks and then carefully pick up a crawdad just behind its pinchers.

I also made mud pies as a child—even tasted them.

I believe it was a ploy by my mother to make me into a girl—about the same time, I started getting pretty things for my room, too—that led to my getting a Betty Crocker Easy-Bake Oven (they still make these). The results from the packaged mixes didn't look much different from my mud pies but, oh, did they taste better (and less gritty). In 1979, that was some good stuff.

I don't have much of a sweet tooth, but I do like savory things, so I have a propensity now to turn almost anything into a small savory cake. My fascination with turning black-eyed peas, okra, or even grits into a small cake might have something to do with my mud pie and Betty Crocker past.

There are the standard cakes out there that you will immediately recognize—crab cakes are one example—but feel free to experiment. Fish cakes and shrimp cakes are easy ones. Legumes are also fun to play with. I first had some black-eyed pea cakes at a restaurant more than ten years ago and they were truly delicious served with a salsa and grilled shrimp.

Cakes like these can be a main course if served with some interesting accompaniments.

And if you want to relive your childhood, let the little ones in on the making of these cakes. They can get their hands dirty in the process of squishing those peas and egg and breadcrumbs together. I promise the results will be much more delicious than the mud pies we used to make during those hot Alabama summers.

Grit Cakes

Sometimes wonderful, wonderful things are created from leftover elements. Artists know this and creative cooks know this. A favorite recipe of mine is one that uses leftover grits. This is a very old Southern recipe that uses leftover grits to make grit cakes, which can then be served for breakfast with syrup drizzled (or if you're seven, poured rapidly until a thick pool covers your plate) on top. I am not certain of the origins but know that it has been around for a long time—especially in my family— although often when I ask other "old" Southerners about them, to my surprise, they have never heard of the recipe. Maybe this is one of those things that are contained—like on the Galapagos—and never make it to other locations.

The basic premise here is to take leftover grits and let them set up overnight (refrigerate to get cool and firm), then cut them into rectangles or squares, dip in egg and roll in cornmeal, and fry up golden brown. Serve them hot with butter and syrup.

As for me I will take savory over sweet any day and thus take the grit cakes and serve them with a fried egg and a little dash or two of Tabasco. So at my breakfast table there are two versions of this dish—the spicy one for me and the sweet for everyone else.

Another savory idea is to serve them with a light tomato sauce and shrimp. My son says I love leftovers for breakfast and it is true. I turn leftover vegetables into my frittatas in the morning, turn leftover beans also into cakes and serve with a fried egg. It is my chance—breakfast, that is—to relive last night's pleasure in a new form. So I am glad to see, just as my seven-year-old is glad to see anything with syrup in the morning, grits get a second chance in the light of a new day.

Serves 4

4 cups chicken broth or water

2½ cups old-fashioned, stone-ground yellow grits

½ cup heavy cream

½ cup cornmeal

½ cup vegetable oil

Line a 9-inch square pan with wax paper. In a heavy saucepan, bring the broth to a boil and slowly stir in the grits. Simmer, stirring constantly, for 10 minutes. Stir in the cream and simmer, still stirring, another 10 minutes. Season it with the salt and pepper. The grits will be thick. Pour the mixture into the baking pan, smoothing the top with a spatula, and cool. Chill for at least two hours or overnight.

When the grits have cooled, sprinkle cornmeal onto a work surface. Invert the grits onto the cornmeal and remove the wax paper. Cut the grits into four squares and halve the squares diagonally to form 8 triangles. Coat each triangle with the cornmeal. In a heavy skillet, heat the oil over medium heat until hot but not smoking. Fry the grit cakes in batches until golden on both sides (about 3–4 minutes total), adding more oil if necessary to keep them from sticking. Drain them on a paper towel.

Place a couple of grit cakes on each plate. Top with a pat of butter and serve with warm maple syrup.

Goat Cheese Potato Cakes

These potato cakes make a delicious side for steaks or pork roast.

Serves 4–6

6 medium potatoes, Yukon Gold

3 tablespoons fresh parsley, chopped

3 tablespoons green onions, sliced

8 ounces goat cheese, crumbled

2 tablespoons olive oil

Salt and pepper

¼ cup all-purpose flour

Preheat oven to 375 degrees.

Add whole, unpeeled potatoes to medium pot. Fill pot with cold water just to cover potatoes; season cooking water well with salt (it should taste like the sea) and bring up to a boil.

Boil on medium-high heat until potatoes are tender but not overdone, about 10–15 minutes. Drain, peel, and mash roughly with a fork.

When potatoes have cooled enough to handle, fold in fresh herbs, goat cheese and salt and pepper to taste.

Mix until just combined; pieces of goat cheese should still be visible. Form mix into eight 2½ x 1-inch cakes. Flour lightly and set aside.

Add olive oil to a large nonstick pan and bring up to medium-high heat. Add potato cakes and fry until first side is golden brown.

Flip onto other side, fry for another minute, and place in oven to finish warming through, about 10 minutes.

Okra Cakes

Okra is a Southern staple yet a much misunderstood food. Her bad reputation comes from the texture—slimy—she exudes if boiled for a period of time. There's nothing slimy about the vegetable when used in the following method of preparation, which also gives you a wonderful way to use okra besides the standard breading and frying them—although there is nothing wrong with that. If you try these cakes and serve them as a side to any roast meat you won't be sorry you did.

Serves 6

1 cup cornmeal

1 cup self-rising flour

2 teaspoons salt

2½ cups water

1 pound whole okra, sliced into ½-inch rounds

½ cup Vidalia onions, chopped

1 tablespoon vegetable oil

In a large bowl, whisk together cornmeal, flour, and salt. Whisk in water to make a thin batter. Stir in okra and onions.

Over medium heat, add vegetable oil to a cast-iron skillet. Use a small ladle to pour batter onto skillet. Pan

Salmon Cakes (We Called Them Patties)

Everyone, I am certain, has a food that warmly and gently, if not perhaps slightly embarrassingly, takes them back to the dinner table of their childhood. If you are like me and spent your adolescent years in the '70s, then you recall that "gourmet" wasn't a word often used in the average American home. Neither, certainly, was the word "foodie." I am good with that and with my culinary past bespeckled with Campbell's soup cans and casseroles. I am. Nevertheless, I am also proud to say that a great number of classic Southern dishes are experiencing a revival and getting the nod from the culinary world that they deserve, and being uplifted and updated in wonderful ways.

But the meal I sometimes crave, prepare, and thoroughly enjoy every bite of is probably not ever going to experience any such revival, I have to say, and please don't hold this against me or judge me any less of a fresh food champion because I go to this dish so willingly and without shame.

My mom called them "salmon patties," not salmon croquettes or any such fancy name, and they were made from canned salmon. Unless you were lucky enough to grow up in the Pacific Northwest you probably didn't have ready access to fresh salmon in the '70s. Not that I am making any excuses for the fact that I use canned salmon today because, as you know, I could get fresh at any market within five miles of me. I used canned salmon because that is what my mother did. And I loved the result. And even worse you might think than loving salmon patties made this way, and revisiting them this afternoon, is that I, an eight-year-old girl, ate them dipped in . . . ketchup.

Now you might be granting me a little leeway to go back to my childhood comforts and experience this dish—reliving a few unseemly food memories is okay you might think, but a grown-up woman with a sophisticated palette would certainly, I am sure you are saying to yourself, modernize or elevate the "patties" and serve them with a remoulade or a creative aioli of some sort, maybe something with capers or at least a little lemon.

But you would be wrong. I made them today just as my mother did (well, I added a bit of Dijon mustard to the mix) and I did it, I ate them dipped in ketchup.

You are probably thinking you will never ever, ever, eat goat cheese made by a woman who would actually prepare, eat and enjoy such a meal. But I would like to implore you to trust my culinary instincts.

Food for me, I am sure you have heard me say this before but it never hurts to repeat myself, is about emotion. It is about the love and comfort that you feel when someone prepares a meal for you or even when you prepare a meal for yourself. There is succor in it, there is celebration in it. Food is about feeling comfortable coming to the table and not being intimidated because you cannot pronounce chèvre or croquette. I hope you feel the same.

> 1 can red salmon, drained, with skin and bones removed
>
> 1 egg, beaten
>
> 1 teaspoon Dijon mustard
>
> 1 tablespoon green onions, chopped
>
> A dash or two hot sauce
>
> 2 tablespoons all-purpose flour (adding a bit more, if needed, to bind)
>
> Olive or vegetable oil for frying

In a good cast-iron skillet, heat oil over medium hot heat. Combine all ingredients and form into patties. Fry until crispy on both sides, about 3 minutes each side.

Serve with a good remoulade, a nice aioli, or ketchup.

Place drained beans in large bowl. Using hand masher, mash beans coarsely. Mix in green onions, bell peppers, cilantro, garlic, jalapeño, and cumin. Season to taste with salt and pepper. Mix in egg and 2 tablespoons cornmeal.

Place remaining 1 cup cornmeal onto flat surface covered with wax paper. Drop heaping 1 tablespoon of bean mixture into cornmeal; turn to coat. Flatten into ½-inch-thick cake. Repeat with remaining bean mixture and cornmeal, forming 10–12 cakes.

Heat 3 tablespoons oil in heavy large skillet over medium heat. Working in batches, fry bean cakes until firm and crisp, adding more oil as needed, about 6 minutes per side. Drain bean cakes on paper towels. Transfer to platter.

Serve warm with sour cream and your favorite salsa.

should be hot enough to make batter sizzle. Cook until underside is browned, about 3–4 minutes, then flip and brown on the other side. Repeat with additional batter adding more oil to pan as necessary.

Black Bean Cakes

Serves 6

2 15-ounce cans black beans, drained well

6 green onions, finely chopped

¼ cup red bell pepper, seeded and finely chopped

¼ cup yellow bell pepper, seeded and finely chopped

¼ cup fresh cilantro, chopped

2 large cloves garlic, minced

1½ tablespoons jalapeño pepper, seeded and minced

2 teaspoons cumin, ground

1 large egg

2 tablespoons plus 1 cup yellow cornmeal

Olive oil for frying

Hoe Cakes/Johnnycakes

I love these little crispy cornbreads! They date back far into our national history as an adaptation of an original Native American recipe—called ash cakes—as they could be made over a fire. George Washington was said to enjoy these for breakfast. Why they then became a more Southern fare I don't know. They are good for breakfast served like a pancake but I like them as a bread served alongside a main course or soup.

Serves 6

1 cup cornmeal

½ cup all-purpose flour

2 teaspoons baking powder

¼ teaspoon salt

1 egg

1 cup buttermilk

Oil or clarified butter for frying

Pre-heat a cast-iron skillet. Stir the dry ingredients

together in a bowl. Mix in the egg and milk. Spoon the batter into the heated skillet or cast-iron griddle and fry like you would a pancake but till they are a little crispy on each side. Serve with butter.

Corn Cakes

Serves 4

2 tablespoons plus 1 teaspoon extra-virgin olive oil

3 cups corn (from 3 ears corn)

2 green onions, very thinly sliced, divided

2 large eggs, lightly beaten

¼ cup cornmeal

Coarse salt and pepper

2 ounces goat cheese, crumbled

In a large nonstick skillet, heat 1 teaspoon oil at medium temperature. Add corn and half of green onions and season with salt and pepper; cook until vegetables soften slightly, 3–5 minutes. Coarsely purée half of the corn and green onions in food processor. Transfer puréed and other half of whole kernel sautéed corn to a medium bowl and let cool, 5 minutes. Add eggs, remaining green onions, and cornmeal to corn mixture and stir to combine.

Wipe skillet, then heat 2 tablespoons oil on medium. In batches, cook cupfuls of corn mixture until set on bottom, about 3 minutes. Flip and cook until cakes are cooked through, 2 minutes. Transfer to a plate. Sprinkle corn cakes with goat cheese.

Serve these alongside any grilled meats or seafoods during those late summer meals. They can also be served on their own with a little salsa on top as a first course or appetizer.

Shrimp Cakes

This recipe is simply a more unique variation on the classic crab cake. I like them for appetizers especially.

Serves 4–6

16 uncooked large shrimp (about 1 pound), peeled, deveined

1 large egg

1 green onion, sliced

2 tablespoons lime juice, freshly squeezed

1 tablespoon mayonnaise

1 tablespoon fresh cilantro, minced

½ teaspoon hot pepper sauce

½ teaspoon salt

Pinch black pepper, freshly ground

1 cup cornmeal

2 tablespoons (or more) vegetable oil

Coarsely chop shrimp in processor. Add egg, green onion, lime juice, mayo, cilantro, hot pepper sauce, salt, and pepper. Blend in using on/off turns. Add 1 cup cornmeal and blend in using on/off turns. Form mixture into twelve 3-inch-diameter cakes. Heat 2 tablespoons vegetable oil in heavy large skillet over medium-high heat. Working in batches, fry cakes until cooked through and golden brown on both sides, adding more oil to skillet as needed, about 6 minutes. Serve with spicy mayonnaise.

Dipping Sauces for Cakes

Spicy Mayonnaise
1 cup mayonnaise

2 tablespoons chili garlic sauce (found in Asian food section of grocery store)

1 teaspoon lime juice, freshly squeezed

Combine all ingredients in mixing bowl.

Asian Dipping Sauce
½ cup soy sauce

½ cup rice-wine vinegar

2 tablespoons honey

3 cloves garlic, minced

2 tablespoons ginger from ginger root, minced

2 teaspoons sesame oil

Whisk together all of the ingredients in a bowl.

Salsa
6 Roma tomatoes, chopped

4 cloves garlic, minced

2 jalapeños, seeded and minced, plus 2 jalapeños, roasted, skinned and chopped

½ red onion, finely chopped

1 tablespoon olive oil

1 lime, juiced

Chili powder, salt, and pepper, to taste

Fresh scallions, cilantro or parsley, chopped, to taste

In a bowl, combine all ingredients. Place in refrigerator for 2 to up to 12 hours.

Black-Eyed Pea Cakes

Serves 4–6

1 cup dried black-eyed peas

3 cups water

1 egg, beaten

½ cup onion, finely chopped

3 tablespoons lime juice, freshly squeezed

½ teaspoon hot pepper sauce

1 cup all-purpose flour

⅓ cup goat cheese

1 tablespoon jalapeño peppers, seeded and minced

2 teaspoons (about) olive oil

Salsa, medium-hot, prepared

Place dried black-eyed peas in medium pot. Add enough cold water to cover by 3 inches; let stand overnight. Drain peas.

Return peas to pot. Add 3 cups water. Cover; simmer until peas are tender, stirring occasionally, about 40 minutes. Drain peas, reserving ⅓ cup cooking liquid.

Cook's note: One 16-ounce can of black-eyed peas can be substituted for the dried peas. Begin recipe here; rinse canned peas well before using.

Transfer 1¼ cups peas to processor and purée until smooth, adding enough reserved cooking liquid 1 tablespoon at a time to help blend. Transfer purée to a large bowl. Mix in beaten egg, onion, lime juice, hot pepper sauce and remaining whole peas. Stir in flour. Season with salt and pepper.

Mix goat cheese and jalapeño peppers in small bowl. Let stand 30 minutes.

Preheat oven to 250 degrees. Heat ½ teaspoon oil in heavy large skillet over medium-low heat. Using 1½ tablespoons batter for each pancake, spoon batter into skillet. Cook until batter is almost set, about 3 minutes. Turn pancakes over; cook until cooked through. Transfer pancakes to baking sheet; keep warm in oven. Repeat with remaining batter, adding more oil to skillet as needed, making 24 pancakes.

Spoon salsa onto plates. Arrange 4 pancakes alongside salsa on each plate. Top with goat cheese mixture and serve.

Sides

When I was nine years old I ate spinach by the "can full." What is wrong with that sentence?

It seems strange to me now that growing up in the South most of the vegetables that hit my plate came from a can. I adored spinach but I don't actually recall seeing fresh spinach in the grocery stores until I was an adult. All of the spinach that I ravenously consumed was from a can. This is strange to me because as you know the South has a rich agrarian tradition. I know Julia Child challenged us as Americans to think beyond the soup can in the 1960s and '70s but one would have thought that those industrialized canned creations wouldn't have seeped into the areas of the country that were rich in—if nothing else—fertile soil and a long growing season.

Outside of pondering why that canned food phenomenon occurred, I can only say how abundantly thankful I am that today I can in an instant acquire fresh spinach—whole leaf, baby leaf, on the stalk, or even triple washed—whenever I so desire it at my corner market. What a wonderful thing. And the odds are increasing that my corner market cares enough to source those beautiful leafy greens I love and other vegetables of choice from farms close to home.

It is even funnier to me now that some of the grocery check-out clerks ask, not out of general culinary curiosity but out of the basic necessity to do their job and ring up my purchases, "what is this?!" about my head of garlic or stalk of ginger.

My point is that we have such a bounty of choice in front of us, a wealth of ingredients with which we can play, in our playroom that is a kitchen, that it would be astonishing and sad if we didn't take great advantage of it.

Near my home in north Alabama, we have a local CSA (community supported agriculture) operation, Doe Run Farm, that produces mind-boggling grandeur from their fields. The variety of tomatoes and root vegetables, peppers, greens and twenty-nine varieties of squash will surprise you with colors that you didn't even know Mother Nature had on her palette.

I launched a cooking class entitled Cook the Box just because the bounty from Doe Run Farm was so vast that many were confused about what to do with what they received in their CSA box.

What you put on your plate as a side today can be as colorful and attention-getting as the centerpiece on the plate.

My children, go forth and eat well!

Sautéed Spinach

Serves 2

1½ pounds baby spinach leaves

2 tablespoons good olive oil

2 tablespoons (6 cloves) garlic, chopped

2 teaspoons kosher salt

¾ teaspoon black pepper, freshly ground

1 tablespoon olive oil

Dash soy sauce

Sea or kosher salt, optional

Rinse the spinach well in cold water to make sure it's very clean. Dry the leaves with paper towel or in salad spinner.

In a very large pot or Dutch oven, heat the olive oil and sauté the garlic over medium heat for about 1 minute, but not until it's browned. Add all the spinach, the salt, and pepper to the pot, toss it with the garlic and oil and soy sauce, cover the pot, and cook it for 2 minutes. Uncover the pot, turn the heat on high, and cook the spinach for another minute, stirring with a wooden spoon until all the spinach is wilted. Using a slotted spoon, lift the spinach to a serving bowl. Serve hot.

Creamy Chèvre Slaw

Just like the slaw that you love with pulled pork on a summer afternoon but just with half the mayo and the added cool factor (for your friends and your figure) of goat cheese!

Serves 4

2½ pounds green cabbage, cored and cut into 3-inch chunks, then finely chopped or shredded

1 medium onion, finely chopped

1 large green bell pepper, finely chopped

1 large carrot, coarsely grated

¾ cups mayonnaise

¾ cup goat cheese, softened

⅓ cup cider vinegar

2 teaspoons sugar

Toss all vegetables in a large bowl with 1 teaspoon each of salt and pepper.

Whisk together mayonnaise and goat cheese, vinegar, and sugar, then toss with slaw. Chill, covered, stirring occasionally, at least 1 hour (for vegetables to wilt and flavors to blend).

Creamy Fromage Blanc Deviled Eggs

This recipe was given to me by my friend Ann Railsback, who also submitted it in one of Belle Chèvre recipe contests and received an honorable mention. Makes one dozen filled egg halves.

Serves 8

7 large eggs

1 teaspoon Dijon mustard

4 tablespoons fromage blanc

1½ teaspoons cider vinegar

½ teaspoon Worcestershire sauce

Salt and pepper

Boil eggs. Transfer eggs to ice water; let sit for 5 minutes. Cool.

Peel eggs and cut in half lengthwise. Remove the yolks. Place yolks in a small bowl and arrange the egg white halves on a serving tray.

Mash the yolks with a fork until no large lumps remain. Add mustard, fromage blanc, vinegar, Worcestershire sauce and salt and pepper to taste. Mix thoroughly until smooth.

Fill each egg with filling.

Warm Potato and Belle Chèvre Salad

Serves 4

2 pounds potatoes, Fingerling or Yukon Gold, cut in 1-inch dice

1 teaspoon Dijon mustard

¼ cup dry white wine

Clove garlic, minced

Salt and pepper, to taste

¼ cup sour cream

1 medium red onion, diced

¼ cup fromage blanc

½ cup fresh parsley

2 tablespoons olive oil

½ cup Belle Chèvre Confetti

4 tablespoons red wine vinegar

2 tablespoons fresh tarragon

Steam potatoes until tender. Drain and toss with with wine, salt and pepper. Add cheese, onion, and parsley. Stir together remaining ingredients. Toss with potatoes and serve immediately.

Orzo with Peas and Mint

A perfect accompaniment to any spring meal. I like this dish warm or cold, which makes it nice for a picnic.

Serves 8

1 pound orzo, cooked according to package directions

¼ cup olive oil

¼ teaspoon lemon zest

3 tablespoons lemon juice, freshly squeezed

1 cup petite English peas

6 ounces goat cheese

2 tablespoons fresh mint, chopped

¾ teaspoon kosher salt

½ teaspoon black pepper, freshly ground

In a large bowl, combine hot cooked orzo, olive oil, lemon zest, and lemon juice. Add peas, goat cheese, mint, salt and pepper, stirring to combine.

Serve warm or cold.

Black Beans with Goat Cheese and Cilantro Oil

This is a great side dish for a meal of enchiladas or tacos. The cilantro oil adds a touch of elegance to the affair, and any oil that remains can be used to make a salsa or vinaigrette. The leftover beans, if you have any, make an incredible filling for quesadillas the next day.

Serves 6

2 cans black beans, drained

1 small onion, chopped

Clove garlic, minced

3 ounces goat cheese

1 cup fresh cilantro, coarsely chopped

¼ cup plus 2 tablespoons olive oil

½ teaspoon salt

¼ teaspoon black pepper, freshly ground

Purée cilantro, ¼ cup of oil, and salt in a blender or food processor, scraping down sides of blender several times. Pour oil into a sieve set over a bowl and let it drain 15 minutes. Press on the solids, then discard.

Heat two tablespoons oil over medium-high heat and sauté the onion and garlic until tender. Add beans and salt and pepper (add more to taste if desired). Mash with a fork or blend coarsely in a food processor.

Sprinkle warm beans with goat cheese and drizzle with cilantro oil before serving.

Creamy Belle Chèvre Grits with Sun-Dried Tomatoes

Serves 6

2¼ cups chicken broth, low-salt

2 tablespoons (¼ stick) butter

Clove garlic, chopped

½ cup (3 ounces) hominy grits, quick-cooking

¾ cup heavy whipping cream

1 4-ounce jar Belle Chèvre Tuscan Chèvre (drained)

½ teaspoon fresh thyme

Fresh chives, chopped

Salt and pepper

Bring broth, 2 tablespoons butter, and garlic to boil in heavy medium saucepan. Gradually whisk in grits and return mixture to boil, whisking occasionally. Reduce heat to medium-low, cover, and simmer until grits are thick and almost all broth is absorbed, whisking frequently, about 8 minutes. Whisk in ½ cup cream and simmer 5 minutes, whisking occasionally. Whisk in remaining ¼ cup cream and simmer until very thick, stirring often, about 5 minutes longer. Stir in Tuscan Chèvre and thyme. Season to taste with salt and pepper. Cook until cheese softens. Garnish with chives, if desired, and serve immediately.

Asparagus and Green Onion Risotto

This side dish is delicious with Rosemary Roast Lamb (see recipe on page 91).

Serves 4

2 tablespoons butter

¾ cup green onions, chopped

½ teaspoon fresh thyme, chopped

1½ cups uncooked Arborio (short-grain) rice

5 cups low-sodium chicken broth

½ pound fresh asparagus, cut into 1-inch pieces

⅓ cup Parmesan, freshly grated

Garnish: shaved fresh Parmesan

Melt butter in a large heavy saucepan over medium heat; add green onions and thyme, and sauté 1 minute or until onions are soft. Add rice, stirring to coat. Add ½ cup broth, and cook, stirring constantly, until liquid is absorbed. Repeat procedure with remaining broth, ½ cup at a time. (Total cooking time is about 20 minutes.)

Stir in asparagus. Simmer 3–5 more minutes or until asparagus is tender and mixture is creamy. Stir in Parmesan. Serve immediately. Garnish, if desired.

Puréed Cauliflower with Goat Cheese

Serves 4

1 small head cauliflower

Water for steaming

1 teaspoon garlic, minced

2 teaspoons butter

1 teaspoon thyme

1 tablespoon salt

1 tablespoon black pepper

½ cup goat cheese

Discard any leaves that may cling to the stem, then break up the cauliflower head. Make sure all of the pieces are around the same size so that they cook evenly.

Put the cauliflower in a flat-bottomed skillet (with a matching lid) and enough water around the cauliflower so that it is halfway covered. Bring to a boil. Reduce the heat to a simmer, cover tightly and steam until tender.

Once the cauliflower is cooked, turn off the heat. Using a slotted spoon, put about half the cauliflower in the bowl of a food processor. Add the garlic and process quickly in short bursts of five or ten seconds. Scrape down the sides of the processor bowl and add the rest of the cauliflower.

When the cauliflower looks like mashed potatoes, transfer it to a large glass bowl. Add the butter, thyme, salt, and pepper. Mix thoroughly, and then mix in goat cheese.

Mashed Potatoes with Herbs and Goat Cheese

Serves 4

2½ pounds potatoes, Yukon Gold, peeled, cut into 1-inch pieces

5 ounces goat cheese, crumbled

4 tablespoons (½ stick) butter

¾ cup half-and-half

3 tablespoons fresh basil, oregano, parsley, chopped, or substitute your own combination

1 tablespoon garlic, minced

Cook potatoes in large pot of boiling salted water until tender, about 25 minutes. Drain well. Return to pot. Mix in cheese and butter. Mash until smooth. Add half-and-half, herb mixture, and garlic and stir over medium heat until heated through. Season with salt and pepper.

Celery Gratin

Celery, it seems, doesn't get its fair share of time at the table but is most often relegated to Bloody Mary glasses. And that is a shame as it really is a delicious vegetable. I adore this gratin with celery and you will too as a side dish to roast meats.

Serves 6

1 pound celery (8–10 large stalks), peeled and thinly sliced crosswise (about 4 cups)

¾ cup Parmesan, shredded

2 ounces goat cheese

½ cup heavy cream

Coarse salt and pepper

2 slices white sandwich bread

1 tablespoon olive oil

Preheat oven to 400 degrees. In a large bowl, mix celery, ½ cup Parmesan, goat cheese, cream, ½ teaspoon coarse salt, and ¼ teaspoon ground pepper. Divide evenly among four 6-ounce ramekins, packing mixture in firmly. Place ramekins on baking sheet, and cover tightly with aluminum foil. Bake until celery is tender, 35–40 minutes.

Meanwhile, tear bread into large pieces, and pulse in food processor until coarse crumbs form. Add remaining ¼ cup Parmesan, and drizzle with olive oil; pulse just until crumbs are coated with oil, 4–6 times.

Remove aluminum foil from ramekins. Dividing evenly, sprinkle breadcrumb mixture over celery. Return to oven and bake, uncovered, until golden, 8–10 minutes more. Let sit 5 minutes before serving.

Greens Pie

There are some people who you love despite their demeanor. Mark Furstenberg, a baker of some renown from D.C., is a friend of mine who besides being a curmudgeon is really underneath it all a lovely man and most certainly an inspirational cook.

I first met Mark when I was seated next to him at a large table for dinner at the Blackberry Farm in Walland, Tennessee. I hadn't known him for more than 90 seconds when, during the sommelier's speech, he was rolling his eyes and muttering under his breath how much he abhorred all of the laborious minutiae of the wine world. I leaned over to him and quietly, politely, said, "Be nice!"

Apparently he wasn't accustomed to being scolded but liked the spunk of it nonetheless. We became instant friends that weekend debating all the reasons why he was a grump.

He visited my home in Alabama once, on a mission to help me undo much harm I felt had been done to my son when he had been given Kellogg's Pop Tarts and fell in love with them. This had to be corrected and Mark took on the challenge to come and bake a homemade equivalent that would be better than the store-bought. It didn't work, at least not for Kelly.

But what did work is this greens pie he made for me after spotting a rival pie of sorts in the Continental Bakery where the lovely Carole Griffin presides. Mark made me his version and I have been making it ever since.

I have taken a few liberties with his recipe, as his crust recipe, although amazing, is challenging and has some hard-to-find ingredients, in my neighborhood anyway.

I will offer up an easy but delicious crust recipe instead.

Serves 6

Easy Dough Recipe
2½ cups unbleached all-purpose flour

1 teaspoon salt

1 teaspoon sugar

1 cup (2 sticks) butter, unsalted, cold and cut in small pieces

3 tablespoons ice water

Blend flour, sugar, and salt in processor. Add butter and cut in, using on/off turns, until coarse meal forms. Add 3 tablespoons water. Using on/off turns, blend just until moist clumps form, adding more water by ½ tablespoonfuls if dough is dry. Gather dough into ball; flatten into disk. Wrap in plastic; refrigerate 1 hour. (Can be made 2 days ahead. Keep chilled. Soften slightly at room temperature before rolling.)

Cook's note: I will cut the butter in small pats and then freeze. I keep some like this on hand for when a crust might need to come into my life.

On a lightly floured surface, roll 1 dough portion to ⅛-inch thickness. Press into the bottom and up the sides of a 9-inch deep-dish pie plate. Refrigerate for 30 minutes.

Preheat oven to 350 degrees. Prick bottom and sides of dough with a fork. Line with parchment paper and fill with rice, beans, or pie weights.

Bake until crust is light golden brown just around the edges, 12–15 minutes. Let cool.

Remove the paper and pie weights.

Filling
2 tablespoons extra-virgin olive oil

2 medium onions, halved and thinly sliced

1 medium carrot, coarsely chopped

1 large celery stalk

3 cloves garlic, minced

1 bay leaf

1 tablespoon fresh thyme, minced

1 bag (16 ounces) collards, chopped, parboiled, and drained well

1 pound asparagus, ends trimmed and sliced into 1–2-inch pieces

1 bag (5 ounces) spinach

1 bunch green onions, cut into 1-inch pieces

1 (15½ ounces) can chickpeas, rinsed and drained

2 teaspoons kosher salt

1 teaspoon black pepper, ground

3 ounces goat cheese

1 tablespoon Parmesan

1 large egg

Salt and pepper, to taste

Pinch red pepper flakes

In a large, deep sauté pan, heat olive oil over medium-high heat. Add onions, carrot, celery, and garlic. Cook until vegetables are soft, approximately 6 minutes. Add bay leaf and thyme, stirring to combine. Add collards, asparagus, spinach, green onions, chickpeas, salt and pepper. Cook until liquids cook off, approximately 10 minutes. Remove from heat, and let mixture cool. Remove and discard bay leaf.

In a small bowl, stir together cheeses and egg. Add mixture to greens, stirring well to combine. Season with salt and pepper and red pepper flakes to taste. (If the greens mixture has excess liquid in the bottom of the bowl, drain it before adding to the crust.)

Spoon filling into prepared pie shell.

On a lightly floured surface, roll remaining portion of dough to ⅛-inch thickness. Carefully place over the top of the filling, pressing dough to edges of the pie plate to seal. Cut an X in the top of the dough to vent.

Bake until crust is golden brown, approximately 20–30 minutes.

Steamed Okra with Lemon Butter

An amazingly simple and delicious side dish.

Serves 4

1 pound medium okra pods

1 tablespoon butter

½ teaspoon salt

1 tablespoon lemon juice

Rinse the okra thoroughly in cold water. Place into steaming basket over 1–2 inches of boiling water. Cover and cook until tender, but crisp, about 5 minutes. Toss with butter, lemon juice, and salt. Serve warm.

Fennel Goat Cheese Mash

This is a side dish par excellence. It goes well with any meat, braised or roasted. The potatoes in the recipe help to smooth the purée, which beats plain mashed potatoes any day. Its slightly exotic aroma will have guests begging for the recipe.

Serves 4

3–4 bulbs fennel, depending on size

2 potatoes, peeled and cut into fourths

2 tablespoons olive oil

2 teaspoons salt

¼ teaspoon black pepper, freshly ground

3 ounces goat cheese

⅓–½ cup whole milk or heavy cream

Preheat oven to 400 degrees.

Trim the tops off of fennel, discard. Cut each bulb into quarters.

Toss with the olive oil and salt and pepper, and roast in the oven on a baking sheet until tender and beginning to brown, about 30 minutes.

Meanwhile, boil a pot of salted water, and cook potatoes until tender, 8–10 minutes.

Purée fennel, potatoes, and goat cheese in a food processor, drizzling milk or cream until desired texture is achieved. Season to taste, if necessary.

Grilled Brussels Sprouts with Goat Cheese

Serves 4

4 cups fresh Brussels sprouts

2 tablespoons extra-virgin olive oil, divided

Salt and pepper

1 tablespoon good-quality balsamic vinegar

4 ounces goat cheese, crumbled

Preheat the barbecue to medium-high heat. Using a small paring knife, cut the stem end of a Brussels sprout and peel away the outer leaves. Continue to cut the stem end of the sprout to allow each layer of leaves to be peeled away without ripping the leaves. Repeat this process with all of the sprouts.

Toss the sprout leaves with 1 tablespoon of olive oil in a large bowl. Season to taste with salt and pepper. Place the leaves on the grill. If the grill grates are too far apart to hold the sprout leaves, place the sprouts in a grill basket. Grill the leaves, turning with tongs to ensure the leaves cook evenly and do not burn, until the leaves are crisp-tender and slightly charred, about 5 minutes.

Toss the grilled leaves with the remaining 1 tablespoon of olive oil and the balsamic vinegar in a large bowl to coat. Crumble the goat cheese over the salad and toss gently.

Mound the salad in a serving bowl or on a small salad platter and serve warm.

Roasted Carrots

Delicious as an accompaniment to roasted meats.

Serves 6

3 pounds small carrots with tops

1 tablespoon olive oil

¾ teaspoon salt

¼ teaspoon pepper

Preheat oven to 450 degrees. Peel carrots, if desired. Trim tops to 1 inch.

Toss carrots with oil, salt, and pepper. Place on a 17 x 12-inch jelly-roll pan.

Bake at 450 degrees for 20 minutes, stirring once. Reduce heat to 325 degrees and bake, stirring occasionally, for 15 minutes or until carrots are browned and tender.

Roasted Sweet Potatoes with Honey and Belle Chèvre Glaze

Serves 6

2¼ pounds red-skinned sweet potatoes (yams), peeled, cut into 1½-inch pieces (about 7 cups)

6 tablespoons (¾ stick) butter

3 tablespoons honey

1 teaspoon fresh lemon juice

8 ounces goat cheese

Preheat oven to 350 degrees. Arrange sweet potatoes in 13 x 9 x 2-inch glass baking dish. Stir butter, honey, and lemon juice in small saucepan over medium heat until butter melts. Pour butter mixture over sweet potatoes; toss to coat. Sprinkle generously with salt and pepper. Bake sweet potatoes until tender when pierced with skewer, stirring and turning occasionally, about 50 minutes.

Asparagus Ribbon Salad with Goat Cheese

Raw asparagus? The idea might sound strange, but when you toss delicate ribbons of asparagus in with a dressing made of olive oil and lemon juice, they begin to soften and take on almost a buttery quality. The texture, along with the acidic bite, is a perfect match for goat cheese. Expect clean plates, even from the most anti-salad eaters.

Serves 4–6

1½ pounds green asparagus, jumbo or regular

3 teaspoons lemon juice, freshly squeezed

1 tablespoon extra-virgin olive oil

1 tablespoon packed mint chiffonade

¼ teaspoon kosher or sea salt

⅛ teaspoon black pepper, freshly ground

2–3 ounces goat cheese

Using a vegetable peeler, peel asparagus into ribbons by starting at the crown of the asparagus and pulling lightly downwards to the end of the stalk. Repeat with all asparagus.

Add lemon juice, salt, pepper and olive oil to the asparagus and toss to coat evenly.

Add the mint, tossing to distribute.

Plate the salads (I find this recipe usually makes about 4 servings, depending on size), then sprinkle the goat cheese on top.

2 cups (packed) cheddar, extra-sharp, coarsely grated

1½ tablespoons all-purpose flour

⅔ cup goat cheese, crumbled

Preheat oven to 400 degrees. Butter 11 x 7 x 2-inch glass baking dish. Melt 3 tablespoons butter in heavy large skillet over medium-high heat. Add shallots; sprinkle with salt and pepper. Cover and cook 5 minutes, stirring often. Reduce heat to medium. Cook, covered, until shallots are deep brown, stirring often, about 6 minutes. Meanwhile, cook macaroni in large saucepan of boiling salted water until just tender but still firm to bite, stirring occasionally; drain well. Reserve pan. Bring half-and-half and hot sauce to simmer in same saucepan over medium heat. Toss cheddar and flour in medium bowl to coat; add to half-and-half mixture. Whisk until sauce is smooth and just returns to simmer, about 2 minutes. Mix in pasta. Season with salt and pepper. Spread pasta mixture in prepared dish. Top with shallots, then goat cheese. Sprinkle with pepper. Bake until heated through, about 15 minutes.

Mac and Two Cheeses with Caramelized Shallots

Serves 4–6

3 tablespoons butter, plus more for baking dish

3 cups (about 6) large shallots, sliced

8 ounces small elbow macaroni (2 cups), uncooked

1¼ cups half-and-half

2½ teaspoons hot sauce (such as Cholula)

Belle's Stuffed Portobellos

Serves 6

Marinated Mushrooms

1 cup olive oil

½ cup balsamic vinegar

½ cup reduced-sodium soy sauce

2 cloves garlic, minced

¼ teaspoon coarse kosher salt

¼ teaspoon black pepper, freshly ground

¼ cup Marsala (optional)

4 large fresh thyme sprigs

6 large portobello mushrooms

Filling

1 package (10 ounces) frozen spinach

1 pound button mushrooms

2 tablespoons olive oil

1 cup sweet onion, Maui or Vidalia, chopped

3 cloves garlic, minced

¼ cup plus 6 tablespoons Parmesan,
finely grated

¼ cup dried breadcrumbs, unseasoned

5 ounces goat cheese, crumbled

For marinated mushrooms: Whisk first 6 ingredients and Marsala, if desired, in medium bowl for marinade. Stir in thyme sprigs. Cut stems from mushrooms and place stems in processor. Arrange mushrooms, gill-side up, in 15 x 10 x 2-inch glass baking dish. Pour marinade over mushrooms and marinate 4 hours, turning to coat occasionally.

For filling: Cook spinach according to package directions. Drain; cool. Using hands, squeeze excess water from spinach. Place in small bowl.

Add half of button mushrooms to processor with portobello mushroom stems. Using on/off turns, process until coarsely chopped. Transfer to medium bowl and repeat with remaining mushrooms. Heat oil in heavy large skillet over high heat. Add onion; sauté until beginning to brown, stirring often, about 3 minutes. Add garlic and stir 30 seconds. Add chopped mushrooms, sprinkle with salt, and increase heat to high. Cook until almost all liquid evaporates, stirring often, about 8 minutes. Season mushroom mixture with salt and pepper. Transfer to large bowl; cool to room temperature.

Add spinach, ¼ cup Parmesan, and breadcrumbs

to mushroom mixture; toss to distribute evenly. Add goat cheese and toss gently to distribute evenly. Season filling to taste with salt and pepper.

Cook's note: Can be made 2 hours ahead.

Cover filling and let stand at room temperature.

Preheat oven to 400 degrees. Transfer marinated mushrooms, with some marinade still clinging, to rimmed baking sheet, gill-side down. Roast until beginning to soften, about 15 minutes. Turn mushrooms over. Divide filling among mushrooms. Sprinkle remaining 6 tablespoons Parmesan on top and bake until heated through and cheese begins to brown, about 15 minutes.

Roasted Asparagus with Lemon and Goat Cheese

Serve champagne or Prosecco to add an elegant, light touch to this as a terrific brunch item or summertime side item.

Serves 6

2 pounds medium asparagus, tough ends trimmed

2 tablespoons plus 2 teaspoons olive oil

3 ounces goat cheese, crumbled

2 teaspoons lemon juice, freshly squeezed

1 teaspoon lemon peel, grated

Position rack in center of oven and preheat to 500 degrees. Arrange asparagus on large rimmed baking sheet. Drizzle with 2 tablespoons oil and turn asparagus to coat well. Sprinkle generously with salt and pepper. Roast asparagus until crisp-tender when pierced with knife, about 7 minutes. Arrange asparagus in single layer on platter. Sprinkle with goat cheese. Drizzle with lemon juice and remaining 2 teaspoons oil. Sprinkle grated lemon peel on top. (Can be prepared 1 hour ahead. Cover with plastic wrap. Let stand at room temperature.)

Cornbread Stuffing

Serves 6

Buttermilk Cornbread (see recipe on page 69)

8 bacon slices

5 tablespoons butter

3 cups onions, chopped

2 cups celery, chopped

1 cup shallots, chopped

4 teaspoons dried rubbed sage

1 tablespoon dried thyme

1½ cups pecans, toasted, coarsely chopped

1½ cups chicken broth, low-salt

3 large eggs, beaten to blend

8 ounces goat cheese

Preheat oven to 325 degrees. Cut cornbread into ¾-inch cubes. Place cornbread cubes on baking sheet and toast until dry but not hard, about 15 minutes. Cool. Transfer to large bowl. Cook bacon in heavy large skillet over medium-high heat until crisp, about 6 minutes. Using tongs, transfer bacon to paper towels; reserve ¼ cup bacon drippings in skillet. Cool bacon and crumble. Add butter to bacon drippings in skillet and melt over medium-high heat. Add onions, celery and shallots; sauté just until pale golden brown, about 10 minutes. Stir in sage and thyme. Add to cornbread cubes in bowl. Mix in pecans and crumbled bacon. Crumble in goat cheese. (Can be prepared 1 day ahead. Cover and refrigerate.)

Stir 1 cup chicken broth into stuffing. Season to taste with salt and pepper. Mix in eggs. Moisten stuffing with remaining ½ cup chicken broth. Transfer to greased 8 x 8 x 2-inch baking dish. Bake stuffing in covered dish for 1 hour. Uncover stuffing and bake until top begins to crisp, about 5 minutes longer.

"Kelly Loves Corn" Corn Pudding

Even before Kelly could say the word "corn" he knew he had found something good. On his first visit to Greece when we took him to meet his Papou and Yia Yia at eighteen months old he discovered roasted corn. It is sold along side streets and even highways in Greece at ancient-looking versions of the now hip "food cart." Diminutive women in black clothing hunch over small charcoal grills roasting succulent cobs of corn until their kernels are charred and black.

Kelly, my sisters, and I had just spent a day on the beach and on the way home we stopped for a roasted corn. Unable to get his small mouth and teeth to yield the kernels from the cob, Kelly cried and cried, so much so that I ended up biting off pieces to feed to him, just as a mother bird would do with her young.

My sisters and I laughed all the way home at the absurd strength of the demand for corn and the hilar-

ity of me fulfilling it. Thankfully, Kelly is now able to consume his own roasted corn without any help from his mother.

This is one dish that is always requested by name for Thanksgiving dinner.

Serves 6

¼ pound (1 stick) butter, unsalted

5 cups (6–8 ears) yellow corn kernels, freshly cut off the cob

1 cup yellow onion, chopped

4 extra-large eggs

1 cup milk

1 cup half-and-half

1 cup goat cheese, softened

3 tablespoons basil leaves, fresh, chopped

1 tablespoon sugar

1 tablespoon kosher salt

¾ teaspoon black pepper, freshly ground

¾ cup (6 ounces) extra-sharp cheddar, grated, plus extra to sprinkle on top

Preheat the oven to 375 degrees. Grease the inside of an 12 x 9-inch baking dish.

Melt the butter in a very large skillet and cook the corn and onion over medium-high heat for 4 minutes. Cool slightly.

Whisk together the eggs, milk, and half-and-half in a large bowl. Slowly whisk in the goat cheese. Add the basil, sugar, salt, and pepper. Add the cooked corn mixture and grated cheddar, and then pour into the baking dish. Sprinkle the top with more grated cheddar.

Bake the pudding for 40–45 minutes until the top begins to brown and a knife inserted in the center comes out clean. Serve warm.

Hoppin' John

I grew up with lots of legumes—lentils and black-eyed peas emerged as my two favorites. The latter stars in this dish, which has its origins in west Africa and is a meal in itself eaten in a bowl with a little cornbread on the side.

In the South, Hoppin' John is traditionally served on New Year's Day for prosperity in the year to come. However, I skip the Hoppin' or the John, whichever is supposed to be the rice in this combination, and have my black-eyed peas solo. I see no need to dilute my chances at good fortune with a little rice.

Serves 8

1 tablespoon olive oil

1 large ham hock

1 cup onion, chopped

½ cup celery, chopped

¼ cup green pepper, chopped

¼ cup red pepper, chopped

1 tablespoon garlic, chopped

1 pound black-eyed peas, soaked overnight and rinsed

1 quart chicken stock

1 bay leaf

1 teaspoon dried thyme leaves

Salt, black pepper, and red pepper flakes

3 tablespoons green onion, finely chopped

3 cups white rice, steamed

Heat oil in a large soup pot, add the ham hock and sear on all sides for 4 minutes. Add the onion, celery, green pepper, and garlic, cook for 4 minutes. Add the black-eyed peas, stock, bay leaves, thyme, and seasonings. Bring to a boil, reduce the heat and simmer for 30 minutes, or until the peas are tender but not falling apart, stir occasionally. If the liquid evaporates, add more water or stock. Season to taste with salt, pepper, and red pepper flakes, and garnish with green onions. Serve over rice. Pass hot sauce if desired.

The Last Sweet Bite

Joy Harjo writes, "Perhaps the world will end at the kitchen table, while we are laughing and crying, eating of the last sweet bite."

I kind of like the idea of the world ending at the table—preferably after dessert. The idea of lingering at the table, completely full and happy, and then after all of the goodness is gone, being presented with something sweet is a very good one.

I prefer something simple at the end of a meal not only because I don't care that much for sweets, but also typically I have already eaten more than I should have and skip the dessert anyway.

Oftentimes, I completely forget dessert when I am planning a meal and then have to pop up and look around the kitchen for something I can stir up quickly. An apple tart is simple to make. If bananas are around, caramelizing them Foster-style is also easy. And nothing is much easier and elegant than a divine chocolate lava cake.

I am not much for baking as it requires an exacting nature and mind, which I certainly do not have. It is hard to add ginger to a half-baked cake, you know.

Notwithstanding my personal absentmindedness and take-it-or-leave-it attitude toward sweets, I do know that finishes can be just as important as beginnings and that it is a shame to end a great meal without a good closing.

Nevertheless, what I offer up in this chapter are relatively simple recipes that can be whipped up without much forethought.

As you might imagine, I tend to find a good place for cheese as the last sweet bite. It turns out that goat cheese is one of the most versatile of cheeses and goes easily from breakfast to dessert. Our breakfast cheeses are practically dessert anyway. Spread a honeyed goat cheese on ginger snaps or pound cake and top with macerated fruit, or put out some soft cheeses and fruit of any kind as a dessert plate, and you will have given your guests, with a minimum of fuss, a last sweet bite.

Strawberry and Fromage Blanc Tarts with Balsamic Reduction

Serves 10–12

6 ounces fromage blanc

4 tablespoons honey

1 tablespoon lemon juice

2 tablespoons all-purpose flour

1 egg

1 tablespoon Grand Marnier

Pinch nutmeg

24 mini filo tart shells, prepared

Combine all but flour in food processor. Slowly sift in flour until smooth. Fill 24 individual mini filo tart shells. Bake at 350 degrees for approximately 10 minutes.

Fruit Toppings

2 cups balsamic vinegar

½ pint fresh strawberries, diced

2 tablespoons sugar

Boil 2 cups of balsamic vinegar until reduced by

half. Toss strawberries in sugar. Drizzle with balsamic reduction. Top tarts.

Berry Salad with Belle Chèvre Dressing

Want to make your fruit a little more sophisticated? This is a very simple and elegant way to dress up your fruit—great for your figure and culinary reputation!

Serves 8

Salad
4 cups fresh berries (raspberry, blueberry, blackberry)

Dressing
4 ounces goat cheese

1 teaspoon Dijon mustard

2 tablespoons honey

2 tablespoons champagne or white wine vinegar

2 tablespoons buttermilk

Dash white pepper

Blend dressing in food processor. Toss berries together with dressing and serve in small serving bowls for a healthful and beautiful treat for dessert or breakfast.

Peanut Butter Fromage Blanc Tart with Do-si-dos Crust

I was asked to come up with a dessert using Girl Scout cookies and our goat cheese for the anniversary of the Girl Scouts of Alabama. This turned out to be deliciously simple!

In this recipe, I use fromage blanc as my cheesecake base.

Serves 4

Cookie Crumb Crust
5–6 tablespoons butter, unsalted and melted

2 sleeves Do-Si-Dos cookies, pulsed in a food processor until resembles crumbs

Cream Filling
2 8-ounce containers fromage blanc

2 small eggs, beaten

¼ cup honey

1 heaping tablespoon all-natural peanut butter

Preheat the oven to 350 degrees.

Mix together the cookie crumbs and melted butter. Evenly divide the mixture and press onto the bottom and up the sides of 2 4½-inch tartlet pans or 1 9-inch tart pan with removable bottoms. Bake the crusts for 10 minutes. Cool.

In a large bowl, mix remaining ingredients until

fluffy and smooth, 2–3 minutes. Evenly divide the cream filling among the tart shell(s), smoothing the tops with the back of a spoon or an offset spatula. Bake for 10 minutes.

Remove from the oven and let cool. Place in the refrigerator for a few hours or overnight until chilled completely.

Belle Chèvre Ice Cream with Toffee

Serves 8

1 pint heavy cream

½ cup sugar

¼ vanilla bean, sliced open

4 eggs

¼ cup goat cheese

½ cup crushed hard toffee

Bring the cream, sugar, and vanilla bean just to a boil in a heavy saucepan over medium-high heat. While the cream is heating, whisk the eggs in a medium bowl until broken up. Remove the boiling cream mixture from the heat. Slowly pour ½ cup of the cream mixture into the eggs and continue whisking. Add the remaining ½ cup of cream and mix. Then, pour the egg/cream mixture back into the remaining cream mixture, and stir until thickened, when the mixture coats the back of a spoon. Add the goat cheese and stir until melted (if you have some chunks remaining, don't worry) about 5 minutes. Strain the entire mixture through a fine mesh strainer back into the bowl. This should remove any remaining cheese chunks as well as the vanilla bean. Set the bowl in a cold water bath and allow to cool some, about 5 minutes.

Pour into the ice cream maker, and freeze according to the manufacturer's directions. Add a bit of the toffee immediately, and some after it's thickened. Save a little to sprinkle on top.

Another delicious option is to stir in The Gracious Gourmet Fig Almond Spread instead of the toffee.

Balsamic Roasted Pears with Honey and Fromage

A simple and elegant dessert.

Serves 4

2 tablespoons butter, unsalted

2 firm-ripe Bosc pears, halved lengthwise and cored

3 tablespoons balsamic vinegar

4 ounces goat cheese, cut into 4 pieces, room temperature

¼ cup honey (I recommend Savannah Bee)

Dessert Drinks

Coffee with Bailey's

I typically don't like sweet drinks and am completely content with a beautiful frothy cup of coffee with my dessert or even in lieu of dessert.

However, I was compelled to try Bailey's Irish Cream in my coffee on a very cold day in New York. I was in the city with my well-bred English friend, Suzie Jennings, who at the time was my trainer. Outside of my son and cooking, horses are one of my true passions. I was working with Susie on cross-country jumping and dressage. She had just recently coaxed me into fox hunting for the pure thrill of it—jumping fences at break-neck (literally) speeds in pursuit of adventure.

I drug her up to NYC because I had to ride in Central Park. There was an old standing stable in the city where you could, if with some proof you could handle under English saddle their thoroughbreds, rent the horses and hack out in the park.

It isn't uncommon for fox hunters to carry along a flask in the pockets of their coats on hunts, and true to fashion Suzie had hers along and poured in some Bailey's. "That's disgusting and I won't drink it," I recall saying. But true to my fashion I ate, or rather drank, my words as we poured it into our coffee after our ride. I have never had a better cup of coffee.

1 cup café au lait (see recipe for French Press Coffee on page 20)

¾ oz Bailey's Irish Cream

Stir Bailey's into warm coffee. Enjoy!

Bourbon as Digestif

Digestif is the French word for a drink that's imbibed as an aid to digestion after a meal. Some cultures have liqueurs dedicated just to this specific time of day after a meal. I cannot think of anything better though than a nice small glass of bourbon.

I consider myself extraordinarily lucky to call Julian Van Winkle and his beautiful bride, Sissy, friends. Not only do they make some of the world's best bourbon and rye whisky but they are dear, dear people. I have been able to share their family's bourbon and stories after a number of meals across the South.

Julian is the third-generation bourbon maker at the Old Rip Van Winkle Distillery in Kentucky. His son Preston is the fourth generation and working with his father to carry on their fine traditions.

If you are able to find their bourbon on the finest menus then count yourself lucky, as it is rare and makes a fine after-dinner drink to be sipped.

Many opinions and preferences abound about

how a good bourbon should be served. I will tell you emphatically that this is never with Coke. It's best served neat (poured straight up with no ice), on the rocks (over ice), or with a splash (referring to a splash of water).

I am not sure I have ever seen Julian drink his bourbon any other way but neat. I prefer mine on the rocks.

Whatever your preference enjoy this bourbon slowly and let the conversations flow.

1 ounce Pappy Van Winkle

1 cold Double Old Fashioned glass

Pour bourbon into glass. Swirl and enjoy.

Preheat oven to 400 degrees.

Melt butter in an 8-inch squared glass baking dish in middle of oven, about 3 minutes.

Arrange pears, cut sides down, in 1 layer in butter and roast in middle of oven until tender, about 20 minutes.

Pour vinegar over pears and roast 5 minutes more.

Transfer pears, cut sides down, to serving plates with cheese and spoon some of juices from baking dish over pears. Drizzle pears and cheese with honey and sprinkle with pepper.

Goat-Cheese Cheesecake

Serves 8–10

11 ounces mild goat cheese, softened

¾ cup sugar

Juice from ½ lemon

Zest from 1 lemon

1 teaspoon pure vanilla extract

6 large eggs, whites and yolks separated

3 tablespoons all-purpose flour

Preheat the oven to 350 degrees. Prepare a 6-inch springform pan.

In a medium bowl, combine the goat cheese with the sugar, lemon juice, lemon zest and vanilla and beat at medium speed until smooth. Beat in the egg yolks, two at a time, incorporating them completely before adding the next batch. Beat in the flour at low speed.

In another bowl, using clean beaters, beat the egg whites until firm but not dry. Beat one-third of the whites into the goat-cheese mixture, then gently fold in the remaining whites. Spoon the batter into the prepared pan and bake for about 40 minutes, or until a skewer inserted in the center of the cake comes out clean. Transfer to a wire rack to cool completely before serving.

Chocolate-Smothered Raspberry and Goat Cheese Buttercream Cakes

This recipe came to Belle Chèvre from Beth Royals, who took a first-place award in one of our recipe contests. We were wowed by these little cakes!

These miniature chocolate layer cakes get their richness and depth of flavor from a secret ingredient, goat cheese, used in the decadent raspberry-kissed buttercream frosting. They are easy to make and perfect for entertaining since they can be made in advance.

Serves 6

Cakes
1 cup hot water

1 tablespoon instant coffee

½ cup butter, cut into 1-inch slices

1 cup sugar

1 cup all-purpose flour

½ cup cocoa powder

1 teaspoon baking soda

¼ teaspoon salt

1 large egg

Raspberry Goat Cheese Buttercream Frosting
8 ounces goat cheese, room temperature

¼ cup butter, room temperature

3 cups powdered sugar

¼ cup seedless raspberry jam

Chocolate Ganache
½ cup heavy whipping cream

8 ounces (about 1¼ cups) semi-sweet chocolate morsels

2 tablespoons seedless raspberry jam

Garnish
6 small sprigs mint

Powdered sugar

Handful of raspberries

Preheat oven to 350. Coat a 6-compartment non-stick jumbo muffin pan with cooking spray.

Combine hot water and coffee in medium bowl. Whisk in butter to melt then cool. Stir together sugar, flour, cocoa powder, baking soda, and salt into large mixing bowl. Add coffee mixture and egg. Beat on medium speed with electric mixer until combined, scraping sides down. Pour into prepared pan.

Bake for 23 minutes, or until a toothpick inserted in the center comes out clean. Cool fully in pan. Once cool, run a sharp knife around cakes to loosen. Invert onto cooling rack. Cut in half horizontally with serrated knife then slice rounded tops off cakes to level. Beat all frosting ingredients in medium bowl with electric mixer until smooth.

Turn cakes upside down. Frost middle, tops and sides. Place cakes in freezer. Ten minutes later,

prepare ganache by placing cream in medium bowl. Microwave to a full boil (just over 1 minute). Add chocolate to cream, whisking until smooth then whisk in 2 tablespoons jam.

Transfer cakes with spatula to cooling rack. Place rack over waxed paper and pour ganache over cakes, coating tops and sides while smoothing with an offset spatula. Refrigerate until set (about one hour, or overnight). Serve at room temperature. Garnish with a mint sprig and raspberries. Dust all over with powdered sugar.

Fig and Goat Cheese Tart

Serves 8

2 sheets store-bought shortcrust pastry

8 ounces goat cheese

4 fresh black figs, halved

3 eggs

¾ cup heavy cream

1 tablespoon chives, chopped

½ cup Parmesan, freshly grated

Sea salt and cracked pepper

Preheat oven to 350 degrees. Cut each pastry sheet into 4 squares. Line 8 lightly greased 4-inch round, fluted tart tins with pastry. Trim excess pastry and lightly prick bottom of each. Divide the goat cheese and fig halves between the cases. Place eggs, cream, chives, Parmesan, salt and pepper in a bowl and whisk until well combined. Pour into cases and bake for 25 minutes or until puffed and set. Cool to room temperature and serve.

Goat Cheese Flan with Candied Peanuts

Serves 4

Caramel
¾ cup sugar

¼ cup water

Flan
4 ounces goat cheese

4 ounces cream cheese

⅓ cup sugar

Pinch salt

⅓ cup heavy cream

¼ cup sweet white wine, such as a Sauternes or Muscat

2 eggs

Candied Peanuts
2 cups raw whole peanuts, shelled

1 cup sugar

⅓ cup water

A sprinkle of salt and cinnamon

First, make the caramel by cooking sugar and water over medium-high heat. If the sugar spatters inside the pot, brush down the sides with a water-dipped brush. Continue to cook until caramel reaches a dark amber color. Remove from heat, allowing caramel to cool a bit. Coat the bottom of 4 3¼-inch diameter ramekins with caramel, swirling just a bit up the sides.

To make the flan, blend in a food processor the goat cheese, cream cheese, sugar, salt, cream, wine and eggs for just a minute or so. Pulse just until thoroughly blended. Pour into prepared ramekins. Place ramekins in a baking dish with raised sides, and pour water into the baking dish to halfway up the sides of the ramekins. Bake in the water bath at 325 degrees for 25–30 minutes. Cool and chill overnight.

For the candied peanuts, mix the peanuts with the sugar and water in a wide, heavy-duty skillet. Cook the ingredients over moderate heat, stirring frequently for at least a few minutes, until the peanuts get crusty and liquid begins to crystallize. Lower the heat and continue stirring, scraping up any syrup collecting in the bottom of the pan and turning peanuts to coat with syrup. Tilt the skillet slightly and remove from heat periodically to regulate heat and avoid burning peanuts and to better coat peanuts with

syrup until syrup darkens; if the mixture starts to smoke, remove from heat and stir.

Right before they're done, sprinkle the peanuts with a pinch of salt and cinnamon, stir them a couple of times, then tilt the peanuts out onto a baking sheet. Let the peanuts cool completely, then break up any clumps. Store in an airtight container, where they'll keep up to a week.

To unmold the flans, set the ramekins in about an inch of water that has been simmered and taken off the heat. Leave them there for about a minute. Remove them and run a very thin knife blade or small offset spatular around the rim of each. Invert onto a serving plate giving it a good tap. The flan should slip out easily along with the liquefied caramel sauce. Serve at room temperature, garnished with candied peanuts.

Ginger Snaps with Honey Chèvre and Strawberries

These are super easy to assemble and are always very pleasing.

Serves 8–10

1 pound strawberries, hulled and quartered

¼ cup sugar

1 5¼-ounce package ginger cookies, such as Anna's Ginger Thins

6 ounces Belle & The Bees Breakfast Cheese

In a large bowl, combine strawberries and sugar, tossing together to combine. Let stand at room temperature for 30 minutes.

Top ginger cookies with desired amount of goat cheese and sugared strawberries. Serve immediately.

Lava Cakes

These are deliciously simple chocolate ooooey gooey cakes and I *adore* them!

Serve with real homemade whipped cream—it won't take long—and you will appreciate them even more.

Serves 6

6 1-ounce squares bittersweet chocolate

2 1-ounce squares semisweet chocolate

10 tablespoons (1¼ stick) butter

½ cup all-purpose flour

1½ cups confectioner's sugar

3 large eggs

3 egg yolks

1 teaspoon vanilla extract

Preheat oven to 425 degrees.

Grease 6 six-ounce custard cups. Melt the chocolates and butter in the microwave, or in a double boiler. Add the flour and sugar to chocolate mixture. Stir in the eggs and yolks until smooth. Stir in the vanilla. Divide the batter evenly among the custard cups. Place in the oven and bake for 14 minutes. The edges should be firm but the center will be runny. Run a knife around the edges to loosen and invert onto dessert plates.

Apple Galette

"Galette" is a French term to designate various types of flat, round, or free-form crusty cakes filled with fruits and baked. I like them because all you have to do is fold up the edges of the dough in a rough form, toss in the oven and you have a lovely end result without much fuss.

Serves 4–6

Easy Dough (see recipe on page 113)

1½ pounds Granny Smith apples, peeled, cored, cut into ⅛-inch-thick slices

4 tablespoons sugar, divided

1 teaspoon lemon peel, finely grated

¼ cup apricot preserves

Whole milk

Lightly flour a flat work surface. Roll out dough to ⅛-inch-thick round, 14 inches in diameter. Transfer dough to large greased rimless baking sheet. Chill 15 minutes.

Preheat oven to 400 degrees. Combine apple slices, 2 tablespoons sugar, and lemon peel in medium bowl; toss to blend. Spread preserves over crust, leaving 1½-inch plain border. Arrange apple slices in concentric circles atop preserves, overlapping slightly. Fold plain crust border up over apples, pinching any cracks in crust. Brush crust with milk. Sprinkle crust edges and apples with remaining 2 tablespoons sugar.

Bake galette 20 minutes. Reduce oven temperature to 375 degrees and continue baking until crust is

golden, about 30 minutes longer. Remove from oven. Let stand at least 10 minutes. Cut into wedges and serve warm or at room temperature.

Strawberry-Goat Cheese Ice Cream

Serves 8

8 ounces strawberries, hulled and quartered

2 tablespoons plus ½ cup sugar

2 cups heavy cream

½ cup milk

4 egg yolks

3 tablespoons corn syrup

2 ounces goat cheese

Combine strawberries and 2 tablespoons sugar. Stir to combine. Set aside.

In a saucepan, over medium-high heat, bring cream and milk to a boil.

Prepare an ice-water bath.

In a small mixing bowl, whisk the egg yolks and ½ cup sugar. Slowly pour in some of the hot cream to temper the eggs.

Pour the eggs into the cream and continue to cook for 2–3 minutes, or until the mixture coats the back of a spoon and steam rises from the top.

Whisk the corn syrup and goat cheese and then whisk this mixture into the cream mixture until smooth.

Float your bowl in a bowl of ice water to chill. Empty ice-cream mixture into an ice-cream machine and freeze according to the manufacturer's directions. Keep frozen until ready to use. Serve with macerated strawberries on top.

Index